THE DOUBLE V

A Novel by Carole Eglash-Kosoff

Published by Valley Village Publishing Company

The Double V, Copyright 2020 by Carole Eglash-Kosoff
Cover design by Brandon Devaney
For more information, Contact Carole Eglash-Kosoff at ceglash@aol.com
Website: www.caroleeglashkosoff.com
13 digit ISBN #: 978-1-7923-5301-7

Authors Note

In 2018 a friend, history buff, and fan of forgotten events, mentioned the Double V to me. I researched it extensively and in late 2019 I wrote and produced The Double V as a stage play.

The play was Directed by Michael Arabian and Produced by Leigh Fortier. The Cast and Production Teams were outstanding.

The Corona virus followed and moving the play forward was not a viable option. During our run, we'd been surprised to learn how many people, of all races and ages, had never heard of this moment in our history...a moment that, twenty years later would blossom into the Civil Rights movement and, eventually, today's Black Lives Matter movement.

The story needed to be told!

Prologue

It was a lazy Sunday, a few weeks before Christmas in 1941. In New York city a light rain was falling but it hadn't slowed the rush of holiday shoppers and visitors to the city searching for last minute tickets to see the show at Radio City or searching for that special gift.

Near 35th St. parents lined up with restless children to have their picture taken on Santa's lap up on Macy's mezzanine. The Chicago Bears were trailing the St. Louis Cardinals 24-20 in the 4th Quarter in one of three NFL football games being played that day. And at a Santa Monica beach a late morning overcast blotted out the sun, as a few brave surfers were taking on some gnarly waves.

In the middle of the Pacific Ocean, far to the West, it was barely 8 a.m. At Opana's Kahulu Point, on Oahu's northern coast, Private Joe Lock, U.S. Army Signal Corp, was fiddling with the radar. It was something new and he still couldn't figure out how it worked. It was blipping, he told Lt. Tyler, the officer in charge. Probably the B-17's coming in from the mainland, the officer responded. Forget it! Go have breakfast!

A dozen miles offshore, the morning fog hovered low over a calm ocean. Four Japanese aircraft carriers, the Akagi, the Kaga, the Soryu, and the Hiryu pointed their bows into the wind and the world would never be the same.

Japanese Zeroes lifted into the air and headed east to America's Pacific outpost, the Hawaiian Islands, attacking our military bases on the island of Oahu. Most of the Naval fleet at Pearl Harbor was destroyed, including eight battleships. More than two thousand soldiers and sailors were killed.

The attack was unprovoked. While tensions between the two countries existed, high-level talks were underway In Washington, D.C. to resolve them.

The next day, President Roosevelt declared war on Japan as well as Italy and Germany, countries that had already been battling our European allies.

America mobilized. Factories converted to producing war materiel. Men rushed to enlist...white men. The Army, Navy, and Marines didn't want Negroes. The few that were in the service, and there less than 5,000 enlisted men and only four Black officers, held menial jobs.

In January 1942 a young Negro, James Thompson, in Wichita, Kansas, tried to enlist. He was beaten by a small group of white men. This was a white-man's war, they had shouted. Upset, the young man wrote a letter to the Editor of the *Pittsburgh-Courier*, a large national black newspaper. That letter galvanized a significant part of the country. It championed the adoption of The Double V, a V for victory in the war and a V for victory over racism. The message hit a chord and attracted athletes, movie stars, and liberal organizations, black and white.

By late 1942, under national pressure from the *Courier's* Double V campaign, the government adopted the principal of Proportional Representation, a hundred whites, ten coloreds. More than a million Negro men would serve valiantly in the war.

In 1945 when the war ended, millions of servicemen returned to civilian life, often settling in new suburban housing developments. But the equality black families had expected wasn't there. In Southern California, many new communities, such as Lakewood and Gardena. excluded blacks. Jobs favored whites, and inner-city ghettos evolved.

By the 1960's racial frustrations boiled over and the Civil Rights movement exploded.

And, it had all begun with a letter from a young black man in Wichita, Kansas.

This book is a dramatization of the events of 1942. Many of the individuals were real. Jimmy Thompson's letter has been included in full at the back of the book, just as he'd written it. Proportional representation was real. The anger and actions of the FBI were real. Ira, Frank and Byron Price were real. Erma is based on a woman reporter for the Courier who was instrumental in bringing The Double V to the public's attention. The back stories are fiction. They might have happened.

Enjoy the read. Don't lose the message. Little has changed. Our nation still has failed to deal with racism and economic disparity.

Chapter One

Christmas was in the air. Above a small rural patch of fertile Kansas farm land, small airplanes circled a pair of runways as pilots did 'touch and go's.' It was just outside Wichita, a mostly rural town of a hundred thousand. A small sign announced Cessna Aircraft factory.

Inside a cavernous building all the employees had been assembled around an improvised stage. Some of them held cardboard cups of coffee, others smoked, as Dwayne Wallace, the Company's President, walked to the stage.

"Good morning, and Merry Christmas. Our nation is ending 1941 at war and that means Cessna Aircraft is at war. We've already lost several key employees who volunteered the day war was declared. To the rest, we're glad you are all part of the Cessna family. The Secretary of War and General Curtis LeMay have told me we need to crank up production and do it quickly. That means plenty of overtime, promotions, and hiring. We need more people who want to work somewhere important, so tell your friends. 1942 looks to be the biggest year Cessna has ever had."

Off to one side Jimmy Thompson and his father, Clyde, listened.

"Sounds good, doesn't it, Jimmy?"

"For Dwayne Wallace, maybe. But I don't know, pop. The war, Cessna, college. Suddenly everything in my life is up in the air. It certainly is lots to think about. I'm heading home. Annie is waiting for me and I've got a test to study for. Finals are coming up."

Charlie Simpson, one of Cessna's floor supervisors, was standing nearby.

"What do you think about that, Clyde? Sounds pretty good. We'll probably need to hire more coloreds. We might even find some who can write their name," he laughed. "They're not all college boys like Jimmy here. Smartest dishwasher we've ever had." He laughed and walked off.

Neither Charlie nor Clyde responded. They'd suffered Charlie's racial wise-cracks before. Clyde headed back to work. Jimmy took off his stained apron and walked toward the exit.

Annie, Jimmy's girlfriend, and almost fiancé, was in the kitchen of Jimmy and Clyde's house when he arrived. A small Christmas tree stood in the corner with unopened gifts surrounding it. Three red-knitted stockings hung from the mantel.

"You're home later than normal, Jimmy. Everything OK? I was beginning to worry."

"No, it's all good. They had a big meeting at the factory. Dwayne Wallace spoke to all the employees. Everyone was all patriotic and smiling. Almost like they were happy we were at war so they could build more airplanes and make a lot more money."

"That sounds pretty jaded. I mean, all the factories in the country will be building airplanes and ships and guns for the war, won't they?"

12

"I suppose so."

Jimmy moved around nervously. He turned on the radio, flipped the dial and then turned it off. Annie stared as her boyfriend paced the room. This wasn't the man she loved and she wasn't sure whether to say anything. Finally, she gave in.

"Jimmy, why are you so nervous? What's going on?"

"It's the war. I haven't been able to sleep very much since it started. We go to the movies and they show all these men enlisting and the flags waving and there isn't a single black person anywhere, not in uniform, not in line, not anywhere. It doesn't seem right. So, I made up my mind. I'm going to enlist."

"You're what?"

"I've decided to enlist in the Army. I need to be part of this war. I can't sit on the sidelines. I just can't."

"And what about us?"

"There'll always be an 'us,' but marriage and finishing college have to wait until this war is over."

"Have you told your Dad?"

"No. I know he'll be against it but my mind is made up."

"Jimmy, this isn't the time to do anything rash. Promise me you'll think about it until after the holidays. Talk to your father. Once you decide what you want to do, you won't be able to change your mind."

"I don't think I'll change my mind, but I promise. I won't do anything until after the new year."

"Oh, Jimmy. I'm frightened."

Jimmy took Annie in his arms and held her gently. They'd been sweethearts for nearly three years, Jimmy's senior year in high school. Annie was one year behind. They'd met at a school dance. One turn around the Gym's decorated floor dancing to a Count Basie song, and after that there was no one else for either of them.

Jimmy kept his promise but 1942 was only a few days old when, his mind unchanged, he decided to enlist.

Wichita's Main street was only a few blocks long. The stores that lined both sides of the street catered mostly to white customers. A Rexall drug store was on the corner next to the A & P market. A few doors further the Army had rented an empty space for a Recruitment office. Flags and an 'Uncle Sam Needs You' poster were prominently displayed.

As Jimmy approached, he noticed several young white men gathered in front, talking.

"I can't wait to get to boot camp."

"Screw boot camp. I just want to get away from my old man. He keeps hollering at me to get a job."

"You're both missing the point. I just want to get to fighting krauts. Paris is over there. I want to liberate a few Mam'selles."

"Yeah, they're just waiting for a high school dropout from Kansas to sweep them off their feet."

"But, you see, I'll be in uniform. They won't know."

"Oh, they'll know the minute you open your big yap."

"Hey, look at that nigger coming down the street. You don't suppose he's coming here, do you?"

"Maybe it's Steppin' Fetchit...the colored who's in the movies. You know...Yes, massa, no massa!"

"No, Fetchit is older. Walks bent over."

"Coloreds all look alike to me."

The men grew silent, watching as Jimmy approached.

Jimmy's discomfort increased and his pace slowed as he saw the group staring at him but he refused to turn around. This was too important.

"Hey, kid, what are you doing here?" One of the men asked.

"I came to enlist," Jimmy answered. "Is this the line?"

"For whites! No niggers!"

"You must be bat-shit crazy. Go home!"

"This is a white man's war."

"Look, guys," Jimmy pleaded. "I don't want any trouble. I want the same thing you do. To enlist and help end the war."

"But you see, you ain't the same. We're white. You aren't. It's that simple."

"We plan on lickin' those Goose-stepping bastards and Nips quick so you can just keep on shuckin' your corn."

"I recognize you. You work at Cessna...in the kitchen. That's where you belong."

"And now there's a war and I want to join the Army and help end it," Jimmy said, trying to keep things calm.

"Arm niggers! No damn way. Go home or get back to your friggin' dirty dishes. Either way you don't belong here with us."

The three men began crowding Jimmy, knocking him down, kicking him. Moments later, laughing, they stopped and walked to the Enlistment office. The Recruiting sergeant walked over to Jimmy.

"Go home, kid. The Army's not accepting and enlistments from blacks."

Jimmy picked himself up, stared at the man, turned and slowly limped home.

Once home, Jimmy sat in the dark, sad and confused. Hours passed as he tried, unsuccessfully, to understand what had happened this afternoon.

At some point Annie came in and turned on the lights. She saw a disheveled Jimmy, eye swollen, just sitting. She stifled a scream.

"Oh, my God. Are you alright?"

"I think so."

"But your bruises. Let me get some things and clean you up."

"My trying to enlist in the Army didn't work out to well," Jimmy mumbled

Annie gently wiped the cuts and scratches from Jimmy's arms and legs, waiting for him to explain what had happened.

He spoke slowly. "A bunch of white guys who were there before me kept me away. They wouldn't let me enlist. They don't want coloreds...said this was a white man's army...

things like that. Then they started pushing and shouting racist shit. I fell to the ground and they started kicking me."

"Didn't anyone stop them?"

"The Recruiting Sergeant came out to separate us but then ignored me. As I was walking off, I noticed him patting the white kids on the back like a proud parent."

"That's terrible."

"I finally got myself home, and I've just been sitting, trying to make sense of what happened."

"My God, Jimmy. You relax. Can I get you something to eat?"

"I'm not hungry. My head is still whirling around. Until a few hours ago I thought I was going to be a soldier, fight for my country. It never occurred to me that my country might not want me."

"Jimmy, those people don't represent the whole country? They're just punks."

"I'd like to think that. I guess I've been pretty naive. Volunteer? Sure, glad to have you help us fight this war. Now I have no idea. Are other guys like me going through the same thing? I need to find out...share it with someone. It shouldn't be this way."

"You're sharing it with me," Annie said softly, putting her arm around him. The two of them sat silently holding one another.

The next few days passed without either of them mentioning Jimmy's enlistment trauma. In one way, Annie was relieved. Maybe her lover wouldn't get into the Army after all. Maybe he'd finish college and they'd get married. A lot of 'maybe's'. What she couldn't know was that Jimmy was unable to put the experience out of his mind.

17

A few evenings later Jimmy sat at the dining room table writing. His mind had been so jumbled he hadn't done well on his finals. At the moment he didn't care. What had happened that afternoon was way more important.

He balled up the paper and started again...and again...and again. He showed what he'd written it to Annie, nodded, and made more changes. It took two more days to get it right, to say what he felt. He signed it and addressed the envelope to the Editor, *The Pittsburgh Courier*, Pittsburgh, Pennsylvania.

Sixteen months earlier,
early fall, 1940

Chapter Two

The young girl tried to hide her tears as each of her five brothers demanded a hug and kiss. The men, all tall and a little gawky, ranged from twelve to their mid-twenties. Most wore hand-me-down clothes with patches on the knees or shoulders. Her father, eyes misty, stood back giving his children time to say their farewells.

He'd miss Erma. Since his wife died three years ago, he watched his daughter try to fill in, doing the cooking and trying to teach her brothers how to clean and do the laundry. That hadn't worked out too well. But Erma had more pluck than all the rest of his children. What was it about girls! She had finished near the top of her class and wanted more. The family would have a difficult time holding it together with her gone. But he loved her and he didn't have it in him to deny her.

He hugged his daughter, kissed her tears, and held back his own as she climbed aboard the bus. Her brothers smiled and waved as the Greyhound pulled away, heading for Pittsburgh.

Erma walked the unfamiliar street carrying the old strapped suitcase her brother, Samuel, had found at a Salvation Army store for $.50. She didn't care. She had said her goodbyes to her father and five brothers at the bus station, kisses all around. It was her first time on a large bus. She had grown up in the small town watching as cars, trucks, and busses passed by, wondering where they were going and what it would be like.

Now she was in Pittsburgh. Her high school diploma was safely tucked in a pocket of her purse next to the $20 her father and brothers had scraped together over the years. They had overflowed with mixed feelings, proud that the only girl in the family had graduated from high school, sad that she was leaving.

Erma Chandler was sure that Bessie's Boarding House her father had found for her until she got settled, was somewhere around here. He had said it was close to where she'd be getting off the bus. Oh, well, it was still early afternoon. The trip took only four hours and the sandwich her father made for her had been enough to stop the barking in her stomach.

She missed her family already, especially her five brothers. I mean, who'd pick on her and then give her a peck on the cheek. But the entire last year of school, she knew she'd have to leave. Her father's income as a Minister in a small, mostly black town, was paltry. The depression meant there weren't many jobs for her brothers or most of the other folks. And getting rid of another mouth to feed meant a little more for everyone else.

There were more jobs each month now that factories were making things for the war in Europe. At least for whites. For blacks, not so much. I mean, it was 1940.

Erma turned the corner and stared into a dirty orange sky perforated by plumes of dark smoke billowing upward from the steel mills that seemed to surround her. So many clouds! She was sure they reached all the way to heaven. She wasn't looking when a baseball landed at her feet.

"Hey, kid! Toss the ball over here."

Erma looked toward the voice. A tall, lanky boy was shouting, heading her way.

"Hey, kid! Please! Toss the ball to me."

She could see him more clearly as he approached. He was light-skinned, almost latte colored, with a pencil thin mustache that made him look like a movie star, maybe Rudolph Valentino. He was the prettiest boy she'd ever seen. She stared, her mouth agape.

"You deaf? We'd like our ball back. We're in the middle of a game...and close your mouth. You could catch flies," he laughed.

She continued to stare and then, suddenly, realized she was holding their baseball. Continuing to ignore the boy, she hurled it across the street, past the boy, past the outfield, through the infield and directly to home plate.

"Wow! I've never seen a girl throw a baseball that far. You are a girl, aren't you?"

"That's what my father and all my brothers tell me. You've got white boys playing with you?"

"Sure."

"Whites and blacks allowed to play together in Pittsburgh?

"It's OK in American Legion ball. It's not OK in the schools."

"Never seen that before. How about letting me play? If you liked that throw, you should see me hit."

"We don't play baseball with girls."

"You mean it's OK for whites to play in your game but not girls?"

"You've got it. Everyone knows girls can't play baseball."

"Then everyone knows squat! You think that throw I made all the way to home plate was an accident?"

"Could have been."

"Tell you what! What's your name?"

"Wendall! What's your name, bossy lady?"

"Erma! Erma Chandler. You let me take a couple of swings at bat. If I don't get a clean hit, I'll clean your shoes. If I do, you decide whether I can join your game."

"Well, it's up to the other guys but, why not, it'll give every-one a good laugh."

"They'll laugh until I hit the ball over the head of your outfielder."

They grinned at one another and walked across the street together toward the dirt-covered, make-shift, baseball field as the other players looked on with jeers and laughter.

Erma dropped her suitcase by the bench, took off her coat and dirtied her hands, ignoring the laughter and taunts. Confidently she walked to the plate.

"Cory, don't throw her anything easy," Wendall shouted.

The outfielders moved in, certain a girl couldn't hit a ball very far as Cory, the white pitcher, stared at the strange alien standing at home plate swinging a bat as she waited. His blue eyes smiled mischievously atop a huge dimple as he gave his friend a 'thumbs-up.' He straddled the mound seriously, assessing the young girl one more time as she waited adver-sarily at the plate.

"Would you like me to throw it underhand?" he teased.

"If that's the best you can do."

Cory released the ball…one of his better fast balls. Erma swung and connected. She smiled with satisfaction as the ball flew over the head of the right fielder. The players were stunned as Cory frowned and then broke into full laughter.

"Lucky! Plain lucky," Wendall shouted, clapping his hands and throwing Cory another baseball. "Give her your curve, Cory. Look out, Erma. Cory's curve is the best in our league."

24

Cory moved the ball around in his palm, stretched, and let the ball go. Erma sensed when the ball would bend. She paused the tiniest part of a second and swung. The ball skipped along the ground between the 2^d baseman and shortstop for a base hit.

This time Wendall and Cory and the rest of the squad applauded.

"It helps to grow up with five brothers," Erma said. "Kind of makes you a tomboy for life."

"O.K, you can play 2^d base."

"I'm better at 1st."

"I play 1st. Don't push your luck. And make sure you throw the ball straight."

"It'll be straight. Make sure you catch it."

Four more innings and an hour later the game was over. The players, white and black, patted Erma on the back. She was now a member of the team.

"You certainly hit my best stuff," Cory said, taking off his cleats.

"It was easier knowing you were throwing a curve. If I hadn't known, I doubt I'd have connected."

"Nice of you to say," Cory responded. "C'mon, let's go across the street for a cold drink. I want to know more about Erma Chandler."

Cory, Wendall, and Erma walked across the street and into Dicken's, a small coffee shop. Several tables were occupied, white and black couples chatting. Erma noticed that whites were sitting with whites, blacks with blacks. They stared at her mixed-race trio before returning to their own conversations.

"Tell me the truth, Wendall. Is this girl a ringer you brought in to embarrass us?

"No way! She kidnapped our ball and held it for ransom. Waitress, three large cokes, please. Lot of ice!"

"OK, Erma, 'fess up. Your brothers taught you to hit like that?"

"Mostly Amos, the eldest. He made sure the others let me play, sort of took me under his wing. He's built like a tree. Wanted to play with a semi-pro Negro team but they didn't pay the players, just passed the hat around the crowd. My Daddy needed him at home. I just got here from Fayette. I'm not sure you big city folks have heard of it. Small town! A four-hour bus ride south of here."

"And what brings you to Pittsburgh?" Cory asked.

"I just graduated from High School and I've come to Pittsburgh to get a job. I can type, take some shorthand and I'm smart."

"And modest," Wendall laughed. "I'm a little surprised your parents were OK with your leaving. You must have been a miserable kid at home."

"I was not," Erma laughed, and then added, "My mom died a few years back.".

The cokes arrived, nice and cold. The waitress stared at the handsome white boy with his two colored friends. She didn't need to say anything. Her eyes said it all. Cory ignored her.

"What sort of job you hoping to find?" Wendall asked.

"Jobs are tough to find these days. There's still a depression going on," Cory said.

"Worse for coloreds," Wendall added.

"Even worse for women."

"I know, but I have good office skills and I write stories. I'll take anything to start."

"You may have to," Cory offered. "Office jobs for colored girls are hard to find and they don't pay much. The good

26

paying jobs are working in the mills but the white men get the first chance at those."

Erma was distracted by a middle-age black man bussing dishes. He smiled, teasing with a few of the customers. His left arm was missing below the elbow but he still managed deftly. He stopped at the adjoining table."

"Hi George, how's it hanging?" Wendall said.

"Sam-o, sam-o. You got any tickets for me?" George responded.

"Two tickets. Pirates, Giants. Next week. Don't let me forget."

"Thanks, Wendall. You're the man."

George moved on.

"What kind of job will you be looking for?" Cory said, eager to learn more about this cute girl.

Still thinking about his friend, Wendall interjected. "You see George over there? Lost his arm feeding coal into one of those huge steel furnaces. A piece of red-hot coal. Not a place I'd want to work. It's a shit job, pardon my words, so only blacks will take it or let their families go hungry. He played baseball with us until the accident. Steel company said it was his own negligence and booted him out."

The three watched George move around the cafe, silent in their own thoughts.

"What do you do, Wendall?" Erma asked.

"I'm a sports reporter for the *Pittsburgh Courier*. It's a colored newspaper. One of the largest in the country?"

"They have black newspapers? I had no idea. Imagine that."

"You didn't know there were black newspapers? What kind of backwards world did you grow up in?

"I never thought of Fayette as being backwards. I mean, the town was small but we got a decent education. We even had a movie theater…ten cents, box of Cracker Jacks was a nickel."

"Most big cities have large colored neighborhoods and they have black newspapers. White newspapers rarely include any news about coloreds. The *Courier* even publishes editions in a few other cities."

"Would they ever hire a really smart office girl? I come pretty cheap."

"I'm not sure, but I can ask."

Erma smiled, convinced that Wendall really was the prettiest…maybe not the handsomest, man she'd ever seen.

"Good luck, Erma. I've got to run." Cory stood, threw down two bills for the check.

"Where you headed?" Wendall asked.

"I scored two tickets to see the Pirates play tonight. They're up against the Cincinnati Reds."

"And you didn't invite me, one of your best friends? I mean, I cover sports for the *Courier* and I couldn't get tickets."

"It was either you or this lovely blond I met at my Dad's office. She was just a little cuter than you. What can I say?"

"If Van der Meer is pitching for the Reds, the Pirates will be lucky to score," Erma interrupted. "They can't hit his left-handed curve. It spins and drops from the opposite direction."

The two men looked at this young girl and the certainty of her tone. They stared, shook their heads, and broke out laughing.

"Is there anything you aren't absolutely certain about?" Wendall asked.

"Not much," Erma smiled.

"OK, we'll bet on it. Loser pays for cokes. Now I've got to run." As Cory exited, his eyes twinkling with the pleasure of having met this gamin, he leaned in and kissed Erma lightly on the cheek. She blushed as her hand moved instinctively to her cheek, now warmed by Cory's lips.

She stared at him walking away. "He's nice," Erma said, pulling the last of her Coke through her straw.

"Cory? He just wandered in last year while we were playing. Said he could pitch and, it turned out, he was really good. He and I hit it off, and since then, we've become good friends."

"I don't think I'd ever said more than a dozen words to a white boy in my entire life. Our school had both coloreds and whites, even a few Puerto Rican kids, but everyone pretty much hung with their own crowd."

"Pittsburgh's not much different. Some mixing, but not much. Are you going to be OK? I mean, where are you staying tonight?"

"It's a boarding house. Close, I think," she said, studying a piece of paper from her purse. "Bessie's Boarding House, 650 Fulton Street."

"That is close. C'mon, I'll walk you over."

650 Fulton Street was a tired, 4-story building built a few years after the turn of the century. It looked reasonably well-maintained. A window box of red geraniums was certainly a welcoming sign.

"Looks like this is the place. You gon'na be OK? Want me to come in with you, make sure it's all good?"

"Thanks, but you've already made me feel welcome. Will I see you again?"

"I'll come by tomorrow."

"And you won't forget to ask your bosses about a job for me."

"I won't forget, but don't get your hopes up."

Wendall started to walk away, but suddenly he remembered Cory's exit. He leaned over and kissed Erma's cheek. She smiled.

29

"This is sure a 'kissin' city," she laughed, climbing the flight of stairs.

She opened the door and entered a past she had only read about. Old furniture was strewn casually around the small lobby, antimacassars and lace covered the arms of two sofas framing the room. The entire room smelled of disinfectant. A wind-up Victrola was playing a scratchy record in the corner and a heavy dark black woman, as old as some of the furniture, stopped humming and smiled from behind a small counter. There were pictures on all the walls of a younger, slimmer version of the woman standing there, in cocktail dresses, some with feathers adorning her hair or dress. Erma had a twinge of sadness on what the passage of years could do when a woman's husky voice got her attention.

"You must be Erma. I thought you'd be here hours ago."

"Yes. That was my plan as well, but I caught this baseball and then I hit the ball and these two boys…never mind. Yes, I'm late. I hope it didn't inconvenience you."

"No. But what about a baseball?"

"It's nothing. Just an unexpected welcome to Pittsburgh."

"My name is Bessie Duvier. I own this establishment. We're quiet and we only have twelve rooms," she said, not sure at all whether this scatterbrain would fit in. "We got money sent for you for a week but if you stay longer, maybe we can work out a better rent."

"That would be…"

At that moment the front door swung open and slammed shut again. Standing in front of it, embarrassed, was a pretty girl wearing a pink coat with a faux fur collar and a hat to match. Sarah Blount, barely twenty, stood there, wearing too much make-up, large hoop earrings, and a devilish look on her face.

30

"Sorry, Bessie. I guess the wind caught the door. I'll be more careful next time."

"Uh-huh! Heard that before. You remember two days ago..."

"It was four days, Bessie."

"Whatever! Come here and meet our new border, Erma Chandler. She'll be in Room 12, next to you. Erma, this explosive young lady is Sarah Blount. If I remember, Sarah is from somewhere around Amish country but as far from their quiet style as I am from bein' twenty."

The two girls smiled at one another.

"Sarah, will you take Erma upstairs to her room and maybe explain some of the house rules that are so difficult for you to follow? You won't mind, will you, Erma? I have a guest coming for dinner and I'm not nearly ready.

"Not a problem, Miss Duvier."

"Please call me Bessie. We're informal here."

"C'mon, Erma. Oh, I'm so glad to meet you. I'm sure we'll be friends and we can help one another, and trade clothes and make-up...."

Sarah's voice trailed off as she led Erma up the three flights of stairs.

"One warning," she whispered. "Bessie's guest is an old lecher named Freddie. When she's not around, he'll try to pinch your ass or cop a feel. I've learned to be light on my feet when he's around."

Chapter Three

Wendall was whistling as he entered the front door of the *Pittsburgh Courier*, pausing only long enough to stamp out his cigarette. He could hear the big presses running, finishing the printing of the morning edition. He'd stayed up late to make sure the box score of the Pirates – Reds game would get included. Erma had been right. The Pirates could only put together two runs against Van der Meer. His mind pictured her with her foot on their baseball and he smiled. She's really a pistol.

A dark figure was sitting quietly in the dark.

"Good morning, Wendall."

"Erma? What are you doing here?"

"You were going to speak to your boss about a possible job for me. I wanted to make sure I was nearby."

"It doesn't work that way in a big city. I speak to him and if he agrees, we make an appointment. Eventually you get interviewed."

"But that's too long a process. I want to start work."

"Even if he agrees to interview you, it doesn't mean he's going to say yes. More likely he'll say 'no.' "

"No, he's going to want to hire me."

"What makes you think so?"

"I'm good, really good."

"...and modest."

"Anyway, if you're as good as I think you are, you'll convince him he needs to hire a woman now, specifically me!"

"You're crazy, you know that. And now you've got me driving the bus for a crazy person."

"I'm not crazy. I just know. Go do it! Please. It'll work out. I know it will," she winked as a frustrated Wendall shrugged his shoulders.

Not sure why he was listening to his new friend, he took the steps to the press offices two at a time. It was early and most of the newsroom was empty. His boss, and the paper's Editor, Robert Vann, was often the first one in and the last to leave. He was alone in his office on the telephone.

Robert Vann was an imposing figure in his late 60's, well over six feet with distinguished gray hair atop a furrowed brow. He was a legend in both the Negro and white communities, having built the *Courier* from a local 'rag' to a paper of national stature that reached the majority of America's twelve million Negroes. In exchange those readers supported most positions taken by the *Courier*...and white politicians knew it.

The walls of his office were testimony to his many successes. Pictures with FDR, awards from the city and civic organizations. There weren't many family pictures, but he displayed one, with his eldest son, in a prominent position. Wendall waited politely until Mr. Vann finished his conversation.

"What are you doing in the office so early, Mayor Scully?"

Cornelius Scully was Pittsburgh's mayor, a savvy politician who worked business, union, and racial groups like a fine surgeon. He would be up for election in the spring and

34

was already lining up support from important constituents, including the *Pittsburgh Courier*.

"Yes, I guess we're both early risers. No, I didn't forget. New school dedication, W.E.B Dubois Elementary school, 2 PM. I'll be there. Got time for a drink afterwards? I'd like your help on an important issue. Fine. Have a good day."

"Mr. Vann, got a minute?"

"Sure, Wendall. I see the Pirates dropped another one last night."

"They really aren't much more than a .400 club at best this year."

"It's their pitching. Their bullpen is weak. What do you need?"

"Has the *Courier* ever considered hiring a woman?"

"We hire women. Who do you think keeps this place clean? Printing ink would be everywhere if we didn't keep this place clean. None of us wants to breathe that stuff."

"No, I mean in a typing pool or as a go-fer."

"You guys write-up your own stories, so we don't use a typing pool and the kids we hire to move copy sometimes grow into reporters so we've always used boys. Why the question?"

"I met this young girl yesterday. She's just arrived in town, needs a job, seems terribly bright and energetic and..."

"And you'd like us to hire her?

"Maybe. She's definitely worth interviewing. There's just something different about her. She's says she's a terrific typist and writes stories, and..."

"And you met her how?"

"She ended up playing in our baseball game. She hit the ball out of the park and she made a throw all the way to home plate from the outfield."

"And you want us to hire her so she can play on the *Courier* baseball team?"

"That, too."

"I don't know. Sounds pretty flaky but send her around sometime and I'll talk to her."

"Really. Thank you, Mr. Vann. She's in the lobby...been waiting there since dawn, I guess. I'll bring her right up."

Wendall raced out of the office before Vann could object. He was down the stairs, grabbed Erma's hand, and the two raced back up the stairs. Now out of breath, they paused at the doorway of Vann's office.

"Mr. Vann, here is the girl, I mean, young lady, I wanted you to meet. Erma Chandler!

"Wendall, that was pretty devious. Have a seat, Miss Chandler, as long as Wendall has inveigled this interview which was not on my schedule this morning. Not you, Wendall. I'm sure if Miss Chandler is as bright and full of energy as you've described, neither one of us needs you hovering."

"Of course! Sorry!" Wendall turned red as he backed out of the office.

"And, close the door."

"Yes, Mr. Vann. Yes, sir."

"Can I call you Erma?"

"Of course. And may I call you Robert?"

"No!" he gasped at the girl's brashness. "I'm still your senior, by more than a few years. Mr. Vann will be just fine."

Vann looked at Erma, trying to assess what it was about her that was different.

"My God, you're young. Wendall didn't quite explain that. How old are you?"

"Almost twenty."

"Yes! Almost! A very liberal interpretation of that word."

"But mature…quite mature!"

"Yes, I'm sure. And why do you think I should hire you to work at the *Courier*?"

"Sir, you've built *the Courier* into a circulation of nearly a quarter of a million with editions in several cities. Your editorial policies speak to every Negro in America. I want to be a part of that."

"Did you rehearse that little speech?"

Erma smiled sheepishly. "I did. Did you like it?"

"I did. And how long have you been in Pittsburgh?"

"I arrived yesterday morning."

"So, in one day you managed to impress our Sports writer with your baseball skills and get an interview with the *Courier*. Anything else I should know?"

The phone rang and they both jumped, breaking the moment.

"Excuse me. Oh, put him on. Lionel, good morning. How are you, sir?'

Lionel Smelty was one of the *Courier's* large advertisers. He was also white and the owner of several furniture stores, most in minority neighborhoods. He was a frequent complainer of the paper's stories and editorial policies. Most recently the paper had run a series on usurious interest rates being unfairly charged on consumer Installment contracts. Smelty's stores hadn't been mentioned but their contracts had been subject to complaints for years.

"Lionel, we've been through this before. I can't change *the Courier's* editorial policy to suit an advertiser. OK, I stand corrected. I won't change our policy. No, not even for a double page color spread. Yes, I love you, too. Will I see you at the Kiwanis luncheon next week? Fine!"

37

As Vann hung up the phone, he saw confusion on Erma's face.

"Where were we? Oh, yes. Sorry about that but we try to keep our news as far from our advertisers as possible and sometimes they get upset. You were saying?"

"I'm a good writer. My spelling and typing skills are excellent and I'm willing to work cheap."

"Well, cheap is what we do here. I don't know. A young girl running around a newsroom."

"Mr. Vann, eventually I want to be a reporter. You've got a Sports section. Why not a women's section. Write about things of interest to women."

"It's a novel idea. I know the white newspapers do that. It might get us some new advertisers. OK, we'll try you out carrying copy and see if we can teach you to write like a journalist."

"Yes, sir...the 5 W's...who, what, why, when, and where."

"Right! We'll start you at $15/week."

"I need $20."

Vann blanched. He wasn't use to brash young girls. My God, he thought, if this kid is typical of this younger generation, heaven help us all. Then he laughed. "You are everything Wendall said you were. $18 and no more discussion."

"Yes, sir. $18 will be fine."

Erma exited Robert Vann's office, kissed Wendall on the cheek, and skipped down the stairs. "I'll see you tomorrow, Wendall. Mr. Vann hired me. I told you he would. Thank you! I'm a working girl. Halleluiah!"

6 a.m. the next morning Erma's alarm went off with an ugly cacophonous sound that could be accused of waking

38

the dead. Erma stirred, shut off the alarm and tried to return to sleep before sitting up with a jerk and jumping out of bed. She pulled up the shade and discovered it was still dark out. She dressed clumsily, first putting her skirt on backwards. Yawning, she finished dressing, looked in the mirror and shrugged. It was hopeless. She had changed clothes three times before settling on the same skirt she'd worn the day before but with a different sweater. Her wardrobe was limited and she promised herself she'd buy something pretty to wear when she got her first paycheck.

The corridors of the *Courier* were dark when Erma arrived. The only light was the rising sun struggling with the fog over the Allegheny river and a smoke-filled sky exuding light through a few dirty windows.

It was barely seven when she reached the second floor where she'd been a day earlier. She found an empty desk in the far corner. A few minutes before nine several men slowly dragged themselves in. They looked at Erma, half-hidden in the back, as if she were an alien being that they are happy to ignore until they'd injected their first morning cup of coffee into their system.

"How long have you been here?" Wendall asked, seeing her as he reached the top of the landing.

"Around seven! I couldn't sleep. Where should I sit? When do I get my first story?"

"Whoa! Slow down! Relax! Have a cup of coffee and when the rest of the reporters arrive, I'll introduce you."

"I want to meet Frank Bolden. I read his column while I was waiting. He's a good reporter, isn't he? I mean, he must be. They include his name. Will I get my name on stories I write?"

"No! First, you aren't going to be writing stories, and second, I've been here more than a year and my name doesn't go on the columns I write. I wish they did but Frank Bolden has a following. Some people buy the paper just to read what he's written. He's one of the best, and here he comes now."

Frank Bolden, twenty pounds overweight, but possessing a memory filled with the accumulated minutiae of decades, strolled in, greeting everyone by their first name. Folded in his arm was a box of jelly-filled doughnuts from Fritzi's doughnut shop around the corner. Frank was a fixture at the *Courier* and his column was syndicated to a dozen other papers around the country, including three white papers where no colored paper was available. He had a deep cleft in his chin and his metal rimmed glasses gave him a perpetual look that said I'm interested in what you're saying. He was also known to imbibe in excess on occasion and by the way he was walking, this was one of those morning-afters.

"Frank, got a second? Someone I want you to meet. Frank, this is...."

Wendall never finished his introduction as Frank pushed forward.

"Tom just asked me about the game last night. He should ask you. Don't ask 'ol Frank about sports and don't ask Wendall about news. He don't know shit about news reporting."

"Frank, hold on a second. This is Erma Chandler, our new copy girl."

"Young lady! Erma! How do you do. Have a doughnut. If you want to know whether Frank Bolden is a good reporter, you need to go to the source. Good reporters always go to the source. I'm Frank Bolden. I AM the source so you can believe me when I tell you that I am one hell of a news reporter."

Erma began laughing, taking a doughnut and curtsying politely.

"Frank, as I started to tell you, this is Erma Chandler, our new copy girl and one of your many admirers."

"Does Vann know we've hired a 'skirt'?"

"He hired her."

"Then I worry that he has, indeed, become senile, lost his faculties, despite this young lady's beauty and elan. For you cave dwellers, 'elan' means having energy, style, and flair... panache. Look it up! Does Ira know?"

"Not yet."

"When you introduce her, make certain it's after he's had a good breakfast. Ira's tamer then, less likely to bite."

Erma watched the interplay as if it was a volleyball game and she was the ball. It was odd being discussed in the third person, batted back and forth.

"Now, let me show you where you'll be working," Wendall said as he pulled her away. "Mr. Vann said to start you with two tasks. Read everything the reporters put out. Sometimes their spelling is crap and their grammar worse. Second, we need to get what they write to the copy room to set it in type. When a reporter shouts "copy"...that's you. You are a 'go-fer.' Go for this, go for that. Run, do not walk. Get their story. If you have time, read and edit it. If not, get it to the copy room. Sometimes, when we get close to press time, we just hope the guys hadn't written something that sounds goofy."

"Do I need to worry about Mr. Lewis? I mean, all he can do is fire me before I get my first paycheck."

"You mean you're getting paid?"

Erma nodded.

41

"In U.S. currency? Mr. Vann was obviously impressed."

The shout "copy" bellowed across the room from Frank Bolden's desk.

"That's you," Wendall declared. "Go get it."

"But where's the Press room?"

"Down one floor. Now hurry!"

She rushed back to Bolden's desk and stopped, out of breath.

"Mr. Bolden, if you need anything, I'm happy to be your go-fer."

"Well, you're the cutest go-fer I've ever worked with. Now get this down to typeset. Who knows, it might be worth a Pulitzer."

"Where is typeset?"

"The Copy Room! Second floor, down one level. Go! Go!"

Erma clenched Frank's article tightly in her hand as if it would break. She ran to the elevator, stomped her feet impatiently, finally giving up and opting for the stairway.

There was no doorway when she got to the first-floor landing as she stared into a wide-open typeset area. Her nostrils flared from the acrid stench of black ink.

Four men were setting type from large trays in front of them. Every face was smudged. Each man wore heavy denim aprons and small box caps, equally dirty. Their tray had fifty slots, each slot filled with tiny metal slugs representing an individual letter, number, or character. The men worked speedily, not having to look where the letter they needed lay. Erma stared. There was no music or chatter but the sound of the presses were rhythmic, like symphonic timpani.

"What can I do for you, young lady? We don't like visitors... especially girls who just come in and gawk."

In front of Erma was an old man, short and hunched over, perhaps the size of a tall dwarf, with white hair and tufts of a white beard, wearing an ink-stained apron under which an ink-stained shirt and ink-stained pants could be seen.

"I'm the new copy girl and I was told to bring this article to Sam for typesetting."

"I'm Sam! So, Vann hired a girl. Bad decision. Nothing personal but girls and newspapers don't fit. Anyway, I like runners who are fast but can also edit the copy they're carrying. Reporters can't type worth a shit...pardon my language, or they can't spell...sometimes both."

"I can do both those things, Sam. Try me. "

"I've heard that type of confidence before. Most times it ain't worth a hen's poop. But, OK, take Frank's article and clean it up."

"Now?"

"Not tomorrow. Use that desk. And I need it fast, we're not holding up the presses for Bolden or anyone else."

Erma nodded and moved to the desk. She immediately saw the problem...grammar, spelling. It was part brilliant writing, part gibberish. She gave up making notes in the margins and put a clean piece of paper into the typewriter. Her hands flew. When she finished, she pulled the paper from the typewriter and handed it to Sam.

"There's nothing changed. Didn't I tell you it needed editing?" Sam grumbled, scanning the paper.

"But I did. Here's Frank's original."

Sam compared the two and shook his head. "Well, I'll be damned. A Frank Bolden column never came down here so clean. Maybe hiring a girl wasn't too dumb after all."

"I'll take that as a compliment," Erma said, heading back upstairs.

A few minutes after returning to her desk came another call 'Copy.' It was Tom, the slightly off-beat Entertainment reporter.

"Hi. You yelled 'copy'. My name is Erma, I'm the new copy girl."

"Yes, I heard Wendall explain it all to Frank. I'm Gary Cooper this week. Last week I was George Raft. I do entertainment."

Erma was completely confused. "I don't get it. Are you Gary Cooper or George Raft?"

"Depends how I feel."

"Does it matter that they're both white?"

"Yes, that is a problem. Maybe I should be Eddie Anderson. Anyway, take that copy down to Sam."

Before she could stop laughing at Tom's nuttiness, she began to head downstairs as another cry of 'copy' was heard. Erma rushed to the other side of the room. Paul Pepper, nattily dressed with a red vest, was standing behind his desk, eyes bloodshot with anger, fists clenched.

"I've been shouting 'copy' for nearly ten minutes. Where the hell have you been?"

"I'm sorry. I was picking up a story from Tom and he had me laughing...

"I don't care."

"And, I'm new here and..."

"And I don't care about that either. I know how you wheedled yourself into this job with a smile and no experience. This is a newspaper, not a high school 'sock hop.' What did you do to get this job?"

Erma was baffled by this man's anger. Everyone she'd met since arriving had been so nice.

"Never mind. I don't enjoy working with amateurs so stay out of my way. Now get my story down to type set, ASAP!

"Look, Paul, I'm sorry..."

"Mr. Pepper. Only my friends call me Paul and you sure as hell are not one of them."

"Mr. Pepper, I was just doing what I was told."

"Right, shaking your tight little black ass. Well, now I'm telling you. You watch yourself. Step out of line and I'll make such a stink, Vann will have no option but to kick you back to wherever you came from."

"I'm..."

"Get out of my sight. I have another column to write."

Erma walked away, visibly shaken. She delivered both stories to Sam and returned to her desk, turning her chair to the wall so no one could see her tears. She pulled a hankie from her purse and dabbed her eyes as Frank Bolden walked over.

"Are you OK?"

"I'll be fine."

"Paul was out of line. He'd been counting the days until his nephew came to work. This was going to be his job. The boy worked her last summer...a good kid. Been taking classes at Penn State. You getting this job..."

"I can imagine. Is there something I should do?"

"Not really. Keep your head down and do your job. It'll blow over or it won't. Would you like me to say something to Paul or Vann or anyone else?"

"No, Frank, but thank you."

Bolden returned to his desk. Erma looked up seeing Paul continue to stare at her.

"I won't be intimidated, Mr. Paul Pepper," she said to herself. "Not by you, not by anyone. I got this job; I'm keeping this job and I'll show you I deserve this job. Find your nephew a job somewhere else."

By the end of the day Erma was exhausted. She must have climbed up and down those stairs fifty times, she thought. She entered the lobby of her boarding house tired and dejected.

"You OK, Erma? You look kind of down."

"Hi, Bessie. Just tired. How was dinner with your guest last night? I could smell the roast upstairs."

"Yes, thank you. We had a nice evening. And, Erma, if you want to extend your stay, I can reduce your rent $3 a night. How does that sound?"

"Thank you. I'd like that."

Erma smiled wanly and climbed the flights to her room. She unlocked the door, kicked off her shoes, and flopped onto the bed.

She lay there trying to decide what would be the next article of clothing she'd remove when a knock was followed immediately by Sarah barging in.

"Erma, I heard you come up the stairs. In this place you can hear everything. I even heard one of the girls flush a toilet at four in the morning." Sarah seemed to continue her patter without taking a breath. "And the girl living here before you wasn't very nice. You're nice. I know you are. It's nice to have a new friend to share things with."

"Hi, Sarah. Look, it's nice that you think I'm nice but I just got home from work...first day, and I'm exhausted. Can you give me a few minutes to gather myself and clean up?"

"Oh, sure! But first, I want to show you my new earrings. They're real rhinestones. Smitty, my new boyfriend, gave them to me last night."

Mustering all the sarcasm she could, Erma blurted out, "And what did you give, Smitty?"

"Oh! OH!," Sarah said, finally getting Erma's meaning but not skipping a beat.

"Silly! Aren't they pretty? I'm so glad I got my ears pierced. How was the new job? Did you get promoted yet? Let's go to the Pub around the corner. Maybe we can meet some nice guys"

"I don't think many colored guys go there. Besides, I'm tired. How about you let me nap for 20 minutes and we'll think about going to the Savoy Saturday evening? I heard that Duke Ellington's orchestra might be playing."

"But today's only Wednesday. What should I do until then?"

"Look for a job. Look for a job. Look for a job. Marry Smitty. Your choice. Close the door on your way out."

"Well, you're no fun. I thought we could be real good girl buddies."

The only reply she got was the sounds of Erma's light snoring.

Chapter Four

Erma invited Sarah to Saturday's baseball game, assuring her she'd have her pick of the young good-looking men who would be playing. Erma thought that getting Sarah out of bed before noon would be the most difficult part but waiting for her new friend to figure out what to wear was equally complicated.

Cory was shouting for her to hurry as the teams finished their warmups. Erma pointed Sarah to the small bleachers and it wasn't long before her friend began fantasizing on which of the players would win her heart.

Midway through the game Erma introduced Sarah to Wendall and Cory and several of the other players. They made plans to all go out for lunch when the game was over. Everything was going well. Erma got one hit in the 2^d inning and another in the 6th. In the 9th inning with their team ahead by one run, the batter hit a screaming grounder past Cory. Wendall, now playing 2^d, stabbed at it, turned and threw to 1st but the ball went high. Erma stretched to a few inches past her limit, caught the ball in the web of her glove for a double play and a one run victory. The players all congratulated one another when heads turned and everyone turned silent.

A man, short and heavily tattooed, black as night, came onto the field. It was Smitty, Sarah's boyfriend. He wasn't anything like the way Erma had imagined him. He was swarthy in a way not usually associated with colored men. Smitty worked on a tugboat on the Allegheny River making good money in wages, pocketing twice that for the goods that slipped through the paperwork. Sarah would never know that her new earrings were part of a jewelry shipment that had been sidetracked.

"Smitty, what are you doing here?" Sarah asked, as she instinctively pulled back from her new friends. She had been standing a little too close to the players, hoping that the teasing scent of the expensive perfume Smitty had given her, would do its magic.

"I went to the boarding house. Thought I'd surprise you. They said you were here, so, I guess the surprise was on me."

"I expected to see you later...for dinner, maybe."

"Yeah! But I never expected to see you sitting on your ass, watching a bunch of pansies throwing a ball."

Cory began to intervene when Smitty raised his hand.

"Can't you see I'm having a conversation with my lady, white boy?"

"And can't you see we're just finishing our game? I'm asking you nicely, please take your conversation somewhere else."

"Really? You want to mix it up with me?" Smitty laughed.

"Not really.," Cory responded, matter-of-factly. "We were all going to get some lunch to celebrate our win. If you're Sarah's friend, maybe you'd like to join us?"

"We run in different circles, buddy. Take a powder."

"Hey, I'm trying to be friends here."

"How about I take that baseball and cram it down your throat...friend?"

Smitty moved threatingly toward Cory, the hands at his side balling into fists. Cory didn't back down but he knew this guy could scrape home plate with his face.

"Smitty, we're leaving. Thanks everyone. Erma, have fun. C'mon, Smitty."

For a moment Smitty's eyes continued to sear a hole through Cory but under Sarah's pressure and her voice, he softened and smiled in a way that told Cory he was lucky. The two walked off. The rest of the group breathed a sigh of relief.

"I've had opposing batters stare at me but they only wanted to get a hit, not tear my liver into shreds," Cory muttered. "Good riddance!" He had pitched a 6-hitter and they had won 2-1. Reason enough to celebrate. "Your friend's choices are something you should talk to her about."

"I don't think so. I mean, we share adjoining rooms at Bessie's where I'm living but I'm not her mother."

"Well, I'm ready for something stronger than a Coke. Besides I still owe you for our bet when the Reds beat the Pirates. What do you say? The three Musketeers, you, Wendall, and me?"

"Am I your date or Wendall's?"

"Does it make a difference?"

"If race makes a difference wherever we're going, then it makes a difference whether I have a white date or a white chaperone."

"Can we find a place where it doesn't make a difference?"

"You tell me. You're from Pittsburgh, I'm not."

"I've got it. We'll go to the movies. It's dark so we'll all blend in. I'll buy the tickets. Wendall can buy the popcorn."

"And no necking...just friends?"

51

"Just friends... for now," Cory smiled. "I make no promises for the future."

"Fair enough. Remember I'm just a young girl from a small town."

"Who grew up with five brothers."

"True!"

Chapter Five

Erma and Sarah didn't connect those next weeks. Erma was pretty sure Sarah had been embarrassed by Smitty's aggressiveness but either way Erma's work was keeping her busy and she didn't have time to fret about it.

When she arrived at the *Courier* and climbed the steps to the main Press room that morning something was different. There was an eerie quiet. The usual conversation was gone and even the water cooler crowd was missing.

"Wendall, what's going on?"

"I guess you didn't hear. Last evening, you'd already left, Mr. Vann was getting ready to leave. He had his coat on and suddenly he collapsed. By the time the ambulance got him to the hospital, he was gone. Everyone who works here at the paper is pretty shaken up. Some of them had worked together with Mr. Vann for years. I mean, to them, the *Courier* and Robert Vann were synonymous."

"I'm so sorry. He was such a nice man."

"And a terrific Editor. He built this newspaper to serious national prominence."

As Erma was about to ask what would happen next, Ira Lewis emerged from his office and moved to the center of the room. He didn't need to say a word. Everyone stopped talking and gathered around. He had their attention.

"This is a terribly sad moment for the *Courier* and I'm sure you all share with me the deep loss of our Editor, Publisher, and spiritual leader, Robert Vann. I know what a giant he was. He had been my mentor for more than twenty years, closer than my father in many ways. That being said, he would have reminded us that we've got a deadline to meet. So, please, let's get this evening's edition out. We'll all have time to grieve. Thank you all."

The rest of the week everyone just did their job, reporting the news, laying out each edition and going home at the end of the day. And then there was the funeral. People, white and black, gathered to give their respects for a life well lived. As Erma sat between Wendall and Frank, she saw the love and respect that people had for Robert Vann. The Mayor spoke, Senator Guffey spoke, and finally, Frank Bolden took the stage. As he spoke, tears flowed. That edition of the *Pittsburgh Courier* was printed with a black drape and Frank's comments were printed verbatim on the front page. It was a poetic eulogy.

By the following Monday, Robert Vann had been laid to rest and everyone needed to move forward. They were helped by a sunny spring day. Erma had stopped on her way to work to buys some flowers. She thought that it would cheer up the office and be less fattening than Frank's dough-nuts. Frank was at his desk intently typing a story with his usual three-finger style as she walked by. She put the flowers in a small vase and set them on his desk. He looked up and they both smiled sadly.

"Frank, got a second?

"Sure, my girl. What's on your mind?"

"I read a bunch of newspapers over the weekend. It seems that there's a lot more stories about the war these days. The British Prime Minister, Neville Chamberlin, resigned and London is suffering terribly from German bombing. All the Jews in Warsaw, Poland, have been locked into a small area. Is America going to get dragged into another European war?"

"Probably, but it isn't clear which side. Liberals like Roosevelt favor helping England and Russia but all the Hearst Newspapers and important people like Henry Ford and Charles Lindbergh hate Stalin more than they hate Adolph Hitler. The odds are probably 8 to 5 that we'll side with England."

"Well, we're a Black newspaper. We're supposed to represent all the Negroes in the country. What do our people want?"

Frank sat back in his chair, took a sip of now-tepid coffee, and tried to organize his thoughts.

"Good question. It isn't clear that either the Stalin or Hitler haters care much what Negroes think. In both their worlds, blacks are just worker bees. What I do know is that if a war starts, I want to be a War Correspondent, see some action."

"And I just want to do some serious reporting," Erma noted. "I've gone through three pair of shoes running copy. I can write if I'm just given a chance."

"Well, Ira has had his hands full taking over from Bob Vann. Be patient."

"Not my strong suit."

Wendall sauntered over to join them. "You two seem very conspiratorial."

"I was asking Frank if he thought we're going to end up in war."

"And Frank thought...?"

"Definitely sooner rather than later," Frank added, looking up from his typewriter. "You know, we did have a division of coloreds in the First World War. I mean, they were treated like shit, but we did have one. Hasn't been much progress since then, has there?"

The conversation ended as Ira Lewis left his office and motioned the reporting staff to gather round.

"Good morning. We need to talk about a couple of things. Mostly I want to make certain that we're all on the same page as far as what stories are important. I don't want us to get lazy and just pull items off the teletype. Is that understood?"

He waited, looking at each of them in turn, making sure he had their attention.

"You've all probably heard the scuttlebutt. I've been moved up to replace Bob Vann...not an easy task with things in the country changing so rapidly. I'm going to need lots of help. Bob wore awfully big shoes. Most importantly, let's all agree on the *Courier's* Editorial priorities. "

Tom spoke up, trying for levity that wasn't going to work.

"Mine are easy. Tell our black readers which movies they'll enjoy, what books are good to read, and what music to listen to...you know, suggestions that help make them a little happier."

"That's fine for you, Tom, although I'm cutting Entertainment down from two pages to one, except on the weekend."

Tom tried to object but he saw the scowl on Ira's face and stayed silent.

"We're going to be part of this war, either supporting one side or the other, or, more likely, getting into it, and we need to report on its effect on the Negroes in this country."

"Ira, with all due respect, war or peace, the same shit has been going on this entire century. Blacks are always sucking hind tit...runt of the litter!" Bolden interrupted.

"And then it all got worse when the depression hit...blacks are the first fired, the last rehired," Wendall added.

This was the first time Erma had been a part of a serious conversation about news reporting. She was developing her own thoughts but she wasn't ready to share them.

Paul, the one reporter who continued to dislike her, chimed in. "Let me give you an example. 80% of the black steelworkers around Pittsburgh only get hired to do the shit jobs like feeding coal into the furnaces."

"There are less than a dozen blacks anywhere in management in this entire state. How do we make that look like rosy progress?" Wendall added.

"You're not telling me anything I don't know," Ira interrupted, reasserting himself. "And I have no interest in soft-selling or bull-shitting our readers into thinking things are rosy out there but what I do know is that war means jobs. Wars need Armies and Armies need guns, airplanes and tanks, and American factories have to build them, so it means jobs."

"Armies also need men...millions of men. That could be good for coloreds as well." Erma was into it with a fervor she'd never felt before at her young age. It only lasted long enough for Frank Bolden to throw water on it.

"The military? They barely think we exist. Last week the head of the Marine Corp said, and I quote "Niggers have no right to serve as Marines. If it were a question of having a Marine Corps of 5,000 whites or 250,000 Coloreds, I would rather have the whites."

"He's a peckerwood. He doesn't speak for the military." Wendall chimed in.

"You sure?" Someone asked as the others voiced their thoughts. Ira let it continue for a few minutes and then stepped in.

"Look, we aren't going to solve this now but I spent nearly an hour on the phone with Senator Guffey. He convinced me that we'll be in this war at some point. He doesn't know when but he thinks it's definitely coming. Meanwhile they're working with all the big industrial companies to shift from making consumer goods to military hardware. Our people need to know where the jobs are and where the prejudice isn't. Meanwhile, we're not changing any of the jobs or priorities that Mr. Vann set up. I want to thank each of you for your outpouring of support. Now get your asses back to work."

The reporters broke into small clusters to continue the conversation as Ira Lewis headed back to his office. Erma, unsure what to do, gritted her teeth and decided to jump headlong into the abyss of the unknown.

"Mr. Lewis...Ira, can I speak with you for a minute?"

"You're the copy girl Bob Vann hired, aren't you? Erma something?

"Yes, sir. Erma! Erma Chandler!" Erma smiled, nervously.

"I've never worked with a woman in the Press room but from all I've seen and heard, you're doing a fine job," he said as he continued toward his office and more important matters.

Like a dog with a bone in its mouth, Erma was unwilling to let the moment pass as she blurted out, "Thank you, but I really want to be a reporter. I can be a good one. I'm sure I can."

Ira laughed, continuing into his office. "I don't think so. People you'd need to interview wouldn't take you seriously. No. Keep doing what you're doing."

Ira tried to close his office door but Erma's shoulder blocked it.

"Mr. Lewis, do you know how many of your 250,000 readers are women?"

"I do not."

"Neither do I, but I'm sure it's a lot. And more women are entering the work force and spending most of the money to maintain the house and children and you should have a woman reporter to report on things of interest to them."

"Uh-huh!" Ira continued laughing as he pushed Erma out of his office and closed his door, leaving the girl flustered and speechless as she stormed back to her desk.

"What are you so riled about?" Wendall asked, as Erma stormed angrily around her desk.

"That man! How dare he close the door in my face?"

"I would guess, and it's just a guess, mind you, that it's because he's the Editor. He kind'a gets the last word. What were you pestering him about?"

"I tried to convince him the *Courier* needed a woman reporter and he should let me do it."

Wendall smiled. It had only been a few months since he'd met this young dynamo but he'd listened to her talk about being a reporter more than once. She was relentless.

"Give it a break! If it's meant to happen, it will."

"Wendall, that's fatalistic bull-crap. It won't happen unless I make it happen."

"OK. OK. Got any plans for the weekend?"

Erma took a deep breath and exhaled, angry at Ira Lewis' rejection. She took a moment before she felt herself under control.

"Sarah and I may go to the Savoy Saturday. Her friend, Smitty, is back on the river, and she's worse at sitting quietly than I am."

"That's a hard comparison to believe. Enjoy! See you Monday!"

As Erma left for the weekend, she stuck out her tongue as she passed Ira's office. He looked up and noticed. Erma panicked and ran out horrified while Ira broke into a huge smile.

Chapter Six

The Savoy Ballroom was set in a neon-filled neighborhood of Pittsburgh's Upper Hill District where the more affluent Blacks lived. On any given weekend you'd be able to hear Duke Ellington or Count Basie or listen to Ella or Billie as a shiny mirrored ball rotated overhead and white jacketed waiters tended the long bar.

Sarah was wearing her most shimmering dress, a red satin with a high flounce in front and thin spaghetti straps that showed plenty of skin. Meanwhile, Erma wore her 'other' dress, a blue floral print. The two girls sat along the wall, listening to the music and watching the dancers. It was still early for the Savoy. Ellington's orchestra wouldn't get on stage for another hour. This early in the evening the Savoy played '78's. It seemed to satisfy the dozen or so couples that preferred to move around an uncrowded dance floor. Most of the dancers were black but white couples were a common sight, taking advantage of the music and the more liberal pouring of drinks at lower prices.

People who wanted to be noticed wouldn't arrive 'til past nine, already rosy-cheeked from the 'one' they'd had at dinner. It was a little bit of a shock when a short, elderly man, already perspiring from his previous dance, asked Sarah to join him in a samba. She'd grimaced a little before taking his sweaty hand and twirling off. Erma laughed to herself when she heard a voice behind her.

"Look who we have here."

It was Cory, Wendall, and a very handsome white stranger. All three men looked very dapper with their bow ties, belted jackets and brown and white Oxford wingtip shoes. Erma smiled, thrilled to see a familiar face.

"My goodness," Erma smiled, "Three handsome men, clean-shaven, bathed, and smelling of Old Spice. What more could a girl ask for?"

"Very funny," Wendall grinned. "Erma, this is my friend, Mack Jackson. He's visiting from Philly. He used to date my sister until she dumped him."

"We are forever arguing who was the dump-or and who was the dump-ee," Mack said.

"Not so," Wendall smiled.

"I dumped her," Mack protested. "Hi Erma, Cory said you were someone I should meet. Apparently, you're his baseball team's secret weapon."

"Do you play?"

'Not really. I'm better at trolling the bleachers looking for pretty girls."

"And, are you scouting for yourself or Cory this evening?"

"Definitely myself.'

'Well, I wish you..."

"Excuse me, you two. I think I see someone who wants to meet me," Mack said as he jolted away as if he were hunting prey. He moved around couples dancing to the center of the dance floor, cutting in on the sweaty man dancing with Sarah.

"I've only read about species of males like that in magazines, living in the wild. I didn't know they really existed," Erma laughed.

"Oh, they exist," Cory smiled. "But they've rarely been domesticated. C'mon, let's you and I dance."

Erma stood, uncertain, as they moved to the dance floor.

"Are you sure this is OK, you and me dancing together?"

"Of course! Why?"

"This is the "other" side of town. A nightclub. Mostly coloreds."

"But the operative word is 'mostly.' "

"And that makes it acceptable?"

"Let's find out."

"OK but you're much more of a risk-taker than I am."

They danced comfortably together. Erma was surprised to realize how good she felt in Cory's arms. He was definitely at ease on the dance floor and she relaxed, following his lead.

"Cory, I just realized this is the first time I've ever seen you without your baseball gear. You're actually quite good looking, for a white boy, I mean."

Cory smiled, and Erma's body tingled in a way she'd never experienced. Better to change the subject, she thought.

"I love the way you throw your curve ball. Let me see your hands. I never looked closely at them."

Cory stretched his hand, never losing the beat of the music.

"They're huge. No wonder you can throw that kind of pitch. You could lose a ball in the palm of your hand and never find it."

"I didn't come here to talk baseball, but my anatomy is at your disposal. You let me know if there's any other part you'd like to see."

Erma blushed as he pulled her closer, spun her around, and dipped her as the music came to an end. She was still blushing when he let go of her and they both applauded the music.

"Cory, I'm not sure you noticed but people are staring at us. Maybe you should find a nice white girl to dance with."

"I'm sure they're staring at us because we're such a handsome couple."

"Yes, that too."

"If you'd rather dance with Wendall, I'll take you over to him," Cory smiled, "Although I'd love one more dance before I relinquish my claim."

"It's your skin."

The band began to play again and the couples across the floor caught the beat. Cory and Erma were into the music and one another, forgetting the world around them.

Off to one side three colored men, all wearing jackets that looked a size too small, watched the pretty young black girl smiling in the arms of that tall, skinny white boy as Sarah, a girl they've seen before, seemed entranced in the arms of a different white boy.

Two of the men left the third and walked separately onto the floor, nudging couples without apology. As the biggest of the three reached Mack and Sarah, he stopped, his arms folded.

"Hey, sweetie, I think this dance is mine."

Mack and Sarah froze as couples near them moved away.

"It's up to the lady, friend," Mack said, gathering himself.

Both men looked at Sarah. She'd rather stay with Mack but she also knew that was fuzzy thinking. The experience of dancing with a polished college white boy instead of sweaty, muscled blacks was both new and exciting. Then she thought of what Smitty's reaction would be and she knew she had no choice. She looked apologetically at Mack and changed partners. Mack smiled and walked off the dance floor toward two young white girls sitting on the far side.

Meanwhile the other black man approached Cory and Erma. When he puffed up his chest, he was the size of a Cadillac. Two buttons popped off his jacket.

"I'm cutting in."

"I don't think so. This young lady is with me."

"It wasn't a question. Whitey, if you want to keep your teeth, I'm cutting in. You go find yourself someone your own color."

Tensions flared as neither man was willing to back down. Erma sensed an ugly scene about to occur. From nowhere Wendall appeared and grabbed Erma's hand.

"Cory, thanks for taking care of Erma while I was in the Men's Room. Are we good here, everyone?"

Cory and the hulk continued to face one another, unconvinced the stand-off had ended.

"You both need to cool it. These people are with me. We're all friends. This is Erma and my name is Wendall. My white friend's name is Cory. I should mention, he's also a YMCA lightweight boxing champion. Anyway, Erma and I both work for the *Courier*. We're a couple...Cory's a friend. OK? No harm, no foul."

"I guess. We just don't like our women being hustled by white boys."

"No hustling! Understood! Now, if we can buy you and your friends drinks, we'll return to our table. You mind if my girlfriend and I finish this dance?"

The man nodded, unclenched his fist and took a step back before returning to his friends. Cory breathed a sigh of relief and Erma smiled as Wendall whisked her off to a swing tune, Dark Town Strutter's Ball.

"Is Cory really a YMCA boxing champ?" Erma asked.

"Hell, no."

An hour later, Mack, Sarah, Erma, Wendall and Cory were sitting together having coffee, laughing at the idea of Cory being a YMCA boxing champion.

"I probably couldn't box my way out of a cardboard box," he said.

"I'm sure they knew that," Wendall said. "It would have taken a lot for them to have started anything but a month ago the reverse took place. Some colored college boys showed up at a dance put on at Temple. They were dancing with white girls and all was good, kids enjoying themselves. A half-dozen or so white kids gathered around and asked them to leave."

"What happened?" Erma asked.

"They left. No one wants a race riot, especially if you're in school. Colleges have been known to expel students from both white and black schools for racial incidents."

"Does it happen often?"

"No, but that's because people in Pittsburgh don't want what's happened in places like Detroit or Mississippi to happen here."

"So, Mack, who was the cute blonde chick you were dancing with?" Cory asked, lightening the conversation.

"She looked young enough to be your daughter," Sarah chided

"Her name is Mabel. She and her sister thought they'd be adventurous. Drove all the way here from Harrisburg. They are way too young. Way too naive."

"Anyway, it's getting late. Sarah, you ready to leave?"

"No, not nearly. I've waited all week for Smitty to be out of town. Let's find an afterhours place."

66

"I know just the right spot," Mack said.

"Of course, you do," Wendall laughed.

Erma frowned but didn't say anything.

"C'mon, Erma. I'll take you home," Cory said, standing

"You sure?"

"I'm sure."

The two said their goodbyes and walked slowly to Erma's boarding house. The night air was pleasant and it was Saturday. They could both relax tomorrow. Erma was having difficulty assessing her feelings, walking alone with a handsome white boy. What would her brothers think? She was pretty sure they'd disapprove. She knew her father wouldn't like it.

As they reached her Fulton Street address, she could see a dim light coming from Bessie's apartment and the strains of a scratched record playing jazz. Erma turned to say good night and thank Cory for bring her home when he put his hand tenderly under her chin, looked into her eyes and kissed her. She met his look without words, surprised but thrilled with a kiss that became mutual the longer it lasted. They both smiled before Erma rushed up the stairs and inside.

Sleep didn't come easy that night. That kiss hadn't just stayed on her lips, it captivated her mind. She propped a pillow behind her head and grabbed some old movie magazines. As she looked at handsome couples out for an evening, she imagined herself partying with them but the more she turned the pages, the more she realized there were no black women in any of the photos.

No, it would never happen. She turned off the light, fluffed her pillow and turned on her side as a tear slipped down her cheek.

Chapter Seven

It had now been more than three years since Ira's divorce. They'd had no children and neither the separation nor the divorce had been amicable. His ex-wife's name was Francine. Francine Tatter before their marriage. She was a tall, independent sort of a woman who had been on her own since she was a teenager. Professionally she was an Interior Designer with wealthy clients from all races and professions. She introduced her new husband to a lot of important people but she couldn't accept playing second fiddle to a husband who was often gone, running off to cover another story. It wasn't the life she'd envisioned or enjoyed, and when she'd asked for a divorce, he'd gone along with it. It left few scars and they'd both moved on.

Since then, he'd dated periodically but there had been no spark. Now, suddenly, this young sprite had come into his life and he was having trouble dealing with it. The upcoming holiday season was making it worse. I mean, who do you give a Christmas present to if it's not someone you care for? But this girl was definitely too young. He understood that, but the heart wants what the heart wants, and he couldn't seem to just let it go.

He moved to his office door and shouted, "Copy!"

He waited for Erma to suddenly appear but there was no response.

"Damn it! Where is that girl? What's her name? Erma! Where is Erma?"

From nowhere, she was there. "I'm sorry, Mr. Lewis. I was editing copy downstairs."

"Editing copy? Why were you editing copy?"

"I've been doing it since I started. Sam complained about the grammar and misspellings in the stories he was getting. He claimed it slowed down the typesetting. Have I been doing something I'm not supposed to?"

"If it helps Sam, I guess it's all right. Damn, I guess there are things going on around here that I'm not aware of. Did Vann know?

"I think so. He knew I could spell and type and write good stories when he hired me."

Ira fidgeted. They'd gotten off on a tangent somehow and besides, she made him nervous. Not in a bad way, but unsettled. That was it, unsettled.

"Come into my office," he stepped aside while she entered and the smell of her body, or her perfume, or whatever, unsettled him even more.

"You've been with the *Courier* six months now."

"Eight months!" she corrected.

"Eight months, right! Are things going well here for you?"

"I love working here but I want to do some real reporting."

"Yes, I'm pretty sure everyone on the staff has heard you say that."

"Probably more than once. I was also thinking of writing up a Letter to the Editor...our Editor, but I'm not sure that would get a reaction either."

"Oh, it might get a reaction, but not necessarily the one you want. The bottom line is that you're a pain in the ass. A sweet one, but definitely a pain where I sit. Everyone likes you. Frank Bolden is certainly on your side. Wendall thinks your magical and Tom thinks you're Lena Horne.

Erma was sure Ira Lewis was going to fire her for being a trouble maker.

"I couldn't carry a song even with a Samsonite suitcase," was the best she could come up with.

"OK. Starting with the new year...my God, it's going to be 1941. I pray it will be a peaceful one. In addition to running copy, you're going to head up a Women's section...maybe a half page each edition...below the fold. I want you to do women's stories, weddings, births, bake sales."

"And Letters to the Editor!"

"Not necessary. Tom does those in his spare time."

"But he doesn't like doing them. He's been giving them to me to do."

"That lazy, no-good...OK, and Letters to the Editor. Now, please, go back to work, and Merry Christmas."

Erma couldn't contain herself.

"Thank you, Mr. Lewis," she said as she kissed him on the cheek and began to leave before turning back. "Do I get a raise?"

"A raise? Hell, no! And call me Ira. Mr. Lewis was my father." The effrontery of this girl.

"But I'll need to dress better if I have to go to weddings..."

"And bake sales..."

"Yes, Mr. Lewis! Ira! And bake sales."

"OK! $25 a week."

"$30.00!"

"$27.00. Now get out of here before I change my mind."

Erma smiled coyly. "Merry Christmas, Ira."

Ira poured himself a drink and sat at his desk, smiling. She's definitely a handful, but working with her constantly running past his door, while a challenge, did feel awfully good.

That Saturday would be the final baseball game of the year, assuming it wouldn't rain. Might be a good time to see if she'd enjoy having dinner with him after the game. It was probably a bad idea but he knew he'd do it anyway.

Saturday was cold and blustery. Ira had come to watch the teams play, hoping he'd have the chance to spend a few minutes alone with Erma but it wasn't working out and he'd gone home.

Erma had convinced Sarah to come out with her once again now that Smitty was out of her life. It seems he'd found someone he fancied more. No great loss as far as Erma was concerned...good riddance. The two girls sat in the coffee shop nursing cups of hot chocolate.

"You know what I like about the rain?" Sarah asked.

When Erma didn't answer, Sarah continued. "It cleans the air. You know what I hate about the rain?"

It was clear her friend didn't need her for a normal conversation, but she thought she'd answer anyway. "It cleans the air."

"No, silly. All the soot from the coal they burn to make the steel dirties all my clothes."

"How do you like your new job, Sarah?"

"Fine, I guess. I'm in the typing pool. But it's all girls. I hate talking to women all day. I need good looking men passing by, throwing looks...flirting."

"Any other black girls in the pool?"

"One. A girl from Howard University. She has a degree in English literature. Imagine! I barely finished high school but here we are, she and I, same lousy job. You got any plans for tomorrow?"

"I do. I'm going to a wedding."

"Anyone I know?"

"I doubt it. Howard and the soon-to-be Lucille Doggeral. It's for a story. I convinced Wendall to escort me. Normally, I'd also have a photographer but the paper bought me a new Brownie Kodak camera. It has an internal flash...no more bulbs, so I'll be taking my own pictures. I've never taken pictures before."

"You should take some pictures of me. You know, just to experiment."

"You're right. Let's do it now. C'mon, you can be my first subject."

Since the game was called, the girls returned to their rooms at Bessie's. Sarah was in her glory, putting on different outfits, different poses, but always smiling at the camera. Meanwhile Erma moved here and there, trying to catch the right light the way she imagined real photographers would do.

Wendall begged off at the last minute so Erma went by herself, wearing a new outfit she'd splurged on. The wedding went without incident and the following Monday she handed the exposed rolls of film to Sam before climbing the stairs to her desk.

Two hours later an angry Sam stood in front of her.

"Is this some kind of a joke? You shot two rolls of film, 24 pictures a roll...that's 48 pictures. I've got five pictures of the bride and groom, eight pictures of the ceiling and the rest of you and some girl."

'That's Sarah. She's my friend. I wanted to make sure I knew how to use the camera before I went to the wedding.'

'And it took 43 pictures to figure it out? Film is expensive and I don't need the extra work. Next time, one roll, no personals. Understood?"

Erma nodded, chagrined.

Sam's tone softened when he realized he had been too stern. "I did like the story you wrote though. I'll set it up proper. You'll be pleased."

Erma sat quietly, not wanting to make eye contact with anyone. Time passed and she could hear the presses begin. She walked to the catwalk over the presses. It seemed like a fantasy that what she'd written had gone from her thoughts to a typewriter and now to an actual newspaper...an almost magical journey.

Erma watched as thousands of papers printed and collated. Ira came and stood next to her. Neither could speak over the noise but they smiled at one another. Ira motioned to one of the pressmen below to bring him two copies of the paper.

He took the papers and led Erma back to his office. He poured them both a small glass of champagne. "To your first wedding and photo shoot!"

"I'm not sure I should celebrate after Sam's dressing down."

"The pictures?"

"You know, don't you?" she asked.

"Know what?" Ira asked innocently.

"You know that Sam left teeth marks in my behind, don't you?"

"Such a vivid description for a dressing down. Yes, I know. Sam is very frugal with the *Courier's* assets, such as film, paper, flash bulbs. Actually, he was relatively gentle with you."

"That was gentle?"

Ira laughed. "Oh, yes! That was Sam being nice."

"Can I see how it all looks in print?"

Erma and Ira opened the newspaper to see the small spread of Erma's first reporting.

"Doesn't fill much space. I thought it would be...'bigger'"

"Actually, it's the amount of space I told Sam to squeeze it into. He wanted to make the photos larger and have a bigger headline."

"Didn't you like what I wrote?"

"Actually, I didn't. You know how to write but I'm not sure you know what to write."

"What do you mean?"

"Lucille Doggeral is now proudly Mrs. Stuart Doggeral, wife and, perhaps, soon, mother. You focused on the woman giving up her job and..."

"Her name...her identity! This is 1941. Women should be able to retain their identity when they marry."

"I'm not ready for feminist causes. Neither is the *Courier* and neither are our readers."

"Are you sure?"

"No, but I am the Editor of this paper. You'll please do it my way."

"Yes, sir," she paused. Leave well enough alone. She couldn't. "But times are changing."

"Anyway, it was just a wedding and the first time we've devoted more than a few words to any women's subject. So, if you want to see more words in print, you'll have to write more stories...and make sure they're in line with *Courier* policies."

"I will. Thank you, Ira." She stood, put down her glass and started to leave before she lost it. Her emotions swung from happy she was in print to displeasure with Ira's reaction to how she'd written the story.

"Relax. Finish your drink. One more thing. You've got a big baseball game this Saturday, if it isn't raining. Reporters against the Press workers. They're tough. How about you have dinner with me after the game?"

He'd been rehearsing how to ask Erma out all week, one half of his brain telling him he was too old for an office flirtation, the other half telling him to go for it. Now it had poured out in a gust of feigned innocence.

"You mean, like a date?" Erma asked. She had worried she might be fired or something and now she was being asked out. That had really come out of left field.

"I guess," Ira fumbled. Had it been months, years, or decades since he actually had to ask a girl out for a date?

"Sure, but you'd have to give me an hour after the game to shower and change."

They smiled at one another, both pleased, but as nervous as two ten-year olds in the flush of their first infatuation.

Some of the staff noticed the color in Erma's cheeks as she returned to her desk. Ira poured himself a drink, lit himself a rare cigar, and sat back in his chair.

Saturday came all too quickly. Each morning that week the entire staff huddled around the teletype to see what the weather forecast. It was the season of unpredictable rain squalls as autumn was getting ready to exit. Everyone had worked late to get the morning edition to bed and printed. It was time to party. It was the day of the big game.

The field had been cleaned, the bases puffed up and the pitcher's mound raked. The entire *Courier* staff huddled in groups, laughing, drinking coffee or dozing in a corner of the seats. Some of the staff had signs made. 'Reporters can write, but they can't hit', 'Inkers are stinkers'. A light rain had fallen during the night and dotted the field, but no one wanted to leave, hoping an ever-peeking sun might yet salvage the game. Flasks and beer bottles could be seen. Erma, Cory, Wendall, and Ira were sitting together. Off to the side Frank Bolden and Sam had their heads together.

"What are Frank and Sam talking about?" Erma asked, her mittened hands carefully sheltering a cup of hot chocolate.

"They're the team managers. Probably trying to decide whether to wait a little longer or cancel because of rain," Wendall responded, jumping up and down to keep warm.

"Whatever you're doing, I hope it's working because you look awfully silly," Erma laughed.

Ira had been standing off to one side, watching his reporters and eyeing Cory.

"I don't think I've met this gentleman. He's not a *Courier* employee," Ira finally asked.

"No," Wendall said, smiling. "Each team is allowed two players who don't work for the paper. We've got Cory and George, over there, tossing balls in the outfield. Rude of me, Ira. This is Cory Phelps. He's a friend of mine. We play on the same team during the year. He's a hell'uva pitcher. Cory, this is Ira Lewis, the paper's Editor in Charge."

"How do you do, Mr. Phelps?"

"Mr. Lewis! Please call me Cory. I'm a big fan of the *Courier*."

"Thank you. Call me Ira. Why?"

"Why what?"

"Why are you a fan of the *Courier*? You look more like a Post-Gazette reader."

"You mean because I'm white."

"Yes. I don't have an exact count but I don't think we have many white readers, although we do have a number of white advertisers."

"Well, let's see. I also read the PG and the New York Times. And I read everything Erma and Wendall write because we're friends and I read most of what Tom writes because I like jazz and swing music and I go to clubs he writes about. And I like Frank Bolden's way of phrasing things...like "from the pot liquor flats to the scotch-and-soda highlands...poor to posh neighborhoods."

"What about the actual news?"

"You mean you print news as well? Sorry, I was kidding. No, not so much. I get that from the PG and Times."

"And your family?"

"Ira, am I being interviewed for a job?"

"No, I'm sorry. It's so rare that I get to speak with someone who's white AND a *Courier* reader."

"That's all right. My father works at Gimbel's. He's an Assistant Controller. I'm getting my Doctorate in History at Carnegie Mellon."

"Your doctorate! That's impressive."

Wendall walked over. "I hate to interrupt but Frank just motioned, the game's been canceled. How about we all go out for a drink?"

"I know a marvelous French restaurant near here that opens early and I haven't had any breakfast," Tom offered. "How about it? Fresh croissants, omelets and an early glass of wine..."

Erma started to speak. She and Ira had made plans to go off somewhere themselves after the game but he intervened, smiling at her.

"Great idea," he said.

The restaurant, Chez Michel, looked French, and smelled French, but the owner and chef was from Jamaica. He was easily 250 pounds with a Caribbean laughter that amplified the French contrast. But that damp fall morning, anything would taste good. Michel's food was exquisite.

Erma took Ira aside. "I don't think this is what either of us had in mind."

"No, but everyone seems to be enjoying themselves. I'm going to leave. We'll try it another time."

"Do you have to?"

"I'd rather. You'll be fine," he said, standing and putting on his coat. "You guys have a good time. See you all Monday."

As he exited, he wanted to turn and see Erma but he forced himself to keep going. He knew there was a sadness on his face. His expectations for the day and the evening had been building. Now they'd evaporated.

Ira walked home slowly, his thoughts a mixture of emotions. He'd already been a failure at his first marriage. He just wasn't good at relationships but he wasn't a hermit either. He missed a woman's smell, her touch and her damned confusing thought patterns. They seemed, too often, to function without logic.

Ira turned the lights on in his apartment even though it was the middle of the day. The sun had never come out. He put a Billie Holliday record on the turntable, poured himself a drink, and stared out the window.

"Face it. You're a lot older than she is."

His spotty image reflected in the window and looked back at him. In his mind's eye he could imagine Erma, in the office, writing, running copy, cajoling for a raise. He smiled. I'm not that much older.

Chapter Eight

Erma checked herself in the mirror. She had splurged on a new suit. It was on sale in the basement department of Gimbel's and had the big shoulder pads that Joan Crawford had made de rigueur. She was off to her first Bake-off assignment. It was in the most affluent Negro section of Pittsburgh, the Upper Hill District. This event would be held in the local high school gym, where it had been held every year since 1934.

A large banner broadcast the Hill District Annual Bake-off. Erma entered. Inside, dozens of tables were set up, women standing behind their creations, each table numbered.

"Good morning," the woman at the reception table smiled, handing Erma a program. "I don't think I've seen you before. Is this your first time?"

"Yes, Ma'am. I'm from the *Pittsburgh Courier*. We're hoping to write an article about your event, with pictures. Will that be alright?"

"Ooh," the woman cooed, "our ladies will be thrilled."

Erma checked her coat but carefully held onto her camera and note pad.

She was nervous. It was her first solo assignment, after the Doggeral wedding debacle, and she was certain everyone around her knew it, laughing silently at the young country bumpkin walking the aisles, overdressed, and under confident.

Erma stopped, took a deep breath to gather herself, and moved forward, stopping to chat with several women. Each woman was urging passers-by to taste their unique baked entry.

Alice Chitterly, a late-40'ish woman with a bouffant hair-do and eyebrows that badly needed plucking, smiled as Erma stopped.

"Would you like to try one of my homemade goodies?"

"Thank you, Mrs...?

"Chitterly! Alice Chitterly! How do you do?"

"My name is Erma Chandler. I'm a reporter from the *Pittsburgh Courier*. We're going to be printing an article about the Hillview bake sale. May I take a photo of you and, what do you call those lovely muffins?"

"Really? I might have my picture in the paper? My goodness, that would be special. My friends will be so jealous. These are my persimmon raisin popovers. My Henry loved them...couldn't get enough. Alice, he'd say, bake some more of those persimmon things I like. I'm a widow...nearly three years right now, but I still hear my Henry telling me he misses my popovers."

"Thank you, Alice. Now stand still, and smile."

A flash popped from Erma's Brownie camera.

"You looked lovely, Alice...thank you so much."

"Me, maybe in the newspaper. Here, Erma, please take a muffin."

"I will, she said, reluctant to upset Alice, standing there, holding this ugly black pimpled 'thing.' "I'll look forward to eating it later."

"At least take a bite now, a small one. I want to see your reaction."

Reluctantly, Erma took a small bite and grimaced a smile. Leaving Alice Chitterly, she rushed to the Ladies Room, throwing up raisins and only heaven and Alice knew what else. Erma threw the balance of the muffin in the trash, rinsed the taste from her mouth, gathered herself, and promised herself she'd be more careful.

She continued walking and photographing. When the winner was announced, Erma was there to photograph Mrs. Nancy Brown, this year's winner, holding her blue ribbon and smiling behind a tray of oatmeal cookies.

Erma spent that evening enjoying a meal of tea and soda crackers, hoping her stomach would accept it as an apology. The next day, she was sitting at her typewriter when Ira and Frank stopped at her desk, laughing.

"What are you two laughing at?"

"Your bake sale story."

"What about it? My stomach thinks it deserves hazard pay."

"The winner, Mrs. Nancy Brown!

"Yes. That was her name. Tall, well put together. Expensive dress! Definitely not 'off the rack.' What about her?"

"You haven't been in Pittsburgh very long but I knew that name sounded familiar," Frank Bolden smiled. "Mr. Brown Is President of the largest Black-owned bank in Pittsburgh. Nancy is his 3d wife and hasn't entered a kitchen since Mr. Brown said 'I do'. Their cook said she bought those cookies at the Giant Eagle market on 6th street."

"Why'd she spill the beans on her boss?"

"$20 and a promise to keep her secret."

"That bitch."

"Don't be sore! Get even," Ira laughed.

"But won't we upset Mr. Brown and his bank?"

"Screw him. He turned us down for a loan two years ago."

"I'm on it, Ira. Thanks, guys."

Chapter Nine

Ira sat alone in his office, staring out at the lights of the city. Everyone had gone. The cleaning crew was doing its thing and the teletype was spitting out stories from around the world that would be transcribed, printed and read at tomorrow morning's breakfast table. Nursing a drink, he picked up the phone and started to dial. Before the first ring, he changed his mind and hung up. He poured himself another drink to gather his courage, picked up the phone and dialed once again.

"Hello, can I speak with Erma Chandler? Tell her it's Ira Lewis. Yes, I'll wait."

It took a few minutes before Erma understood a man was waiting for her on the lobby telephone.

"Hello," she said, curious and out of breath from running down the two flights of stairs.

"Erma? It's Ira."

"Ira. Hi. Is anything wrong?"

"Not really. It can wait until Monday. I'm sorry I called and bothered you. Go back to whatever you were doing."

"No. I'm glad you called. Things are so busy during the day we don't get a chance to actually talk to one another."

"You know, we never had our dinner."

"No, we didn't. I didn't know whether you'd forgotten or lost interest."

"Oh, I didn't lose interest. I wondered if we could reschedule?"

"I'd enjoy that," Erma said, smiling at the thought and warmed by the idea a man she liked was actually asking her out on a date.

"How about tomorrow night...if you aren't busy?"

"If...can you hold a minute?"

"Sure!"

Erma held her hand over the mouthpiece and shouted up to Sarah. Both women had begun keeping their doors open when the other was around to make things seem less lonely.

"Sarah, would you mind very much if I begged off our going to the movies tomorrow evening?"

Sarah moved to the top of the stairs and shouted down. "Why? We were going to see the new Jimmie Stewart movie that came out over Christmas. They say it was swell and...."

"Thanks, Sarah. I knew you'd understand."

"But! Oh, never mind. I can always go with Smitty."

"I'm back, Ira. Sorry for the delay. Yes, tomorrow is good."

"Great. If you feel like a movie besides dinner, I hear that new Jimmie Stewart movie is good."

"How about we talk about it at dinner?"

"Good night."

"Good night, Ira." Erma hung up the phone and climbed the stairs lazily. Sarah waited at the top of the landing, anxious to know what had happened but Erma just smiled, patted her friend's cheek and went into her room, closing the door behind her.

They had dinner at a small, but popular, sea food restaurant along the river. Ira was wearing a 'spiffy' bow tie and tweed jacket. He looked like a Ivy League college Professor. They were both nervous and making conversation at the beginning wasn't very smooth since neither wanted to make it an evening where the entire conversation was the *Courier*. After dinner, they walked along the river.

"That was a nice restaurant. Thank you. I don't usually eat that much."

"It's impossible to not overeat at The Oyster House. They're also one of our good advertisers".

"Is that called mixing dinner and business?"

"Not really. I'd eat there even if they didn't advertise, and, I'm glad you enjoyed it."

"Isn't the river pretty with the moon's reflection."

Ira reached for Erma's hand and she took his easily.

"You're certainly easy to please," he said.

"That's the first time anyone has said that to me. People usually tell me I'm difficult to work with. Someone recently even told me I was a pain in the ass."

Ira smiled. "Yes, but a delightful one, if I recall."

"These are all new adventures for me. Remember, I'm from a small town."

"You've certainly adjusted well. I'm glad Bob Vann hired you."

"Me, too."

Ira put his arm around Erma. "I do like being with you."

She replied with her eyes, resting her head on his shoulder. Moments later, they stopped. He pulled her closer and they kissed.

"I'm sorry, he said, afraid it was too much too fast.

"I'm not," Erma whispered.

Chapter Ten

The next few months flew by. Ira agreed to join Erma for Thanksgiving back in Fayette. He was nervous. He knew he was being showcased to her father and brothers and while he was a decade younger than her father, that still made him a lot older than her family would have preferred. But everyone was on their best behavior and the day went without incident. A week later, Erma moved a toothbrush and pajamas into Ira's apartment.

A quiet Sunday. They both slept late and made love. Ira was exiting the bathroom, having just showered, a towel around his waist while Erma fixed something to eat.

"Cute look!" she laughed at her bare-chested lover, grey hairs beginning to outnumber the brown ones.

The telephone rang and Ira answered.

"Frank? That you. What's up that can't wait until tomorrow? The radio. OK."

Ira hung up the phone and turned on the radio.

Guns, explosions and a panicked reporter all mixed in a cacophony of noise. Japanese planes were bombing Pearl Harbor and military installations throughout Oahu and the Hawaiian Islands. Erma dropped the hot cup of coffee she'd just poured herself and joined Ira in front of the radio.

"I've got to get to the paper," Ira said without emotion.

"I'll come with you."

"No. I need you to call in as many of the staff as you can reach and tell them they're needed. Frank is already there."

Ira sped through the Sunday afternoon traffic ignoring any and all speeding laws. The newsroom was crowded as radio reports were being blared throughout the office. Each report that came in over the teletype was scanned and shown to Ira.

"Sam, get the presses ready," Ira ordered. "We're going to run a special edition. Tom, Paul, Wendall...forget sports and entertainment. Frank, each of you take a story...death toll, surprise attack, how badly was our fleet destroyed. Are we now at war? You guys figure it out."

"Ira, let me do a Home Front story. We had some black sailors and soldiers there, I'm sure."

"Sure, write it up and we'll try and fit it in."

When it was all put to bed, everyone sat around until the paper was printed. There it was. Big, bold headlines! **JAPS ATTACK U.S.**

"Good job, everyone. Go home, hug your families, get some sleep and be back here early tomorrow," Ira said, shaking hands with as many of his tired staff as he could.

As they exited both Wendall and Tom kissed Erma on the cheek. Paul walked by teary-eyed. Erma drifted over to Ira, alone, eyes red, leaning against his office door.

"I've never seen Paul crying before. I didn't know he had a tender side."

"He has a twin brother stationed at Scofield Barracks in Honolulu. He hasn't been able to find out whether the man is alive or dead."

"Oh! I didn't know. How are you holding up?"

"Tired...and a little frightened."

"Of what?"

"I don't really know. I'm pretty sure our lives are going to change in ways we'd never expect, and not all of them good."

They embraced, each of them trying to comfort the other. Finally, their eyes red, they held hands, turning off the office lights as they exited, the teletype continuing to report on the attack.

The next morning, Monday, December 8th, the entire room listened, gripped, to the radio. President Franklin Roosevelt addressed a somber Congress. He spoke of 'a day of infamy' declaring that the United States was now at war. Men and women cried openly, both giving, and seeking comfort.

Those next weeks were numbing. The sinking of the USS Arizona had killed nearly 1,200 sailors, most in a watery grave along with their ship. Eight battleships were lost, the heartbeat of the Navy. Shock was slowly wearing off, replaced with anger as the entire country was coming to grips with the idea of war.

In the *Courier* newsroom, it was no longer business as usual. There would be no more soft news.

Frank and Ira were there early, reading the news flashes coming off the teletype.

"Jesus, hard to believe things could be this bad," Ira said. "We're getting the crap kicked out of us in the Pacific and in Europe."

"We had to expect it," Frank nodded. "We weren't ready for a war. The Japs have an experienced Army and their attack at Pearl destroyed what was supposed to be American dominance in the Pacific. And their Army. They've been fighting the Chinese for three years. Meanwhile the entire world stood by and watched Germany build up its military for nearly a decade without saying a word."

"German tanks are only 100 miles from Moscow and the British are struggling against Rommel's tanks in Libya. Paul! Paul, come over here, please."

"Good morning, guys, anything good going on?"

"Not really, Paul. Did you hear any more about your brother?" Ira asked.

"No. The family is pretty distraught. He's got a wife and two young children living in San Diego. He was supposed to be home for Christmas."

"I'm sorry. How do you feel about writing a short article about him as being typical."

Paul nodded.

"Frank, anything interesting at your end? I've got Tom writing domestic news. Wendall is still doing sports but I figure sports is going to take a back seat to the war."

"Actually, sports may turn out to be a mixed bag. Yogi Berra and Ted Williams have already said they'll be enlisting...even Hank Greenberg. The biggest name, of course, is Joe Louis, our own Brown Bomber. I'm already working on that story."

"Tom is finding the same thing with popular musicians. They've already announced Glenn Miller will be heading up the US Army Air Force band."

"I took this item off the wire a few hours ago," Paul said, holding up the teletype story. A young black kid in Wichita, Kansas, was beaten up by some white kids when he tried to enlist. They kept shouting that this is a white man's war, wouldn't let him sign up."

"That's pretty much true, isn't it?" Frank added.

"I guess. I never did figure out why my brother thought it was ok for blacks to be soldiers. They aren't treated any better in the Army than as civilians."

"Might be because no other decent jobs were available."

"Paul, write it up, give it 800 words or so," Ira said. "Now, what about blacks? Where are we in all this? We need some black heroes! Black accomplishments."

"Erma found a story," Wendall chimed in. "A good one, I think. Erma, join us."

"Erma, Wendall says you've got a good human-interest story."

"I think so. A young black kid, Dorie Miller, one of the few coloreds in the Navy, was a cook serving on the USS Nevada battleship docked at Pearl Harbor. He was below when the Japs attacked. He comes to the deck and sees white sailors lying dead everywhere. He climbs up onto an antiaircraft gun, moves a dead body aside and begins shooting. Downs four Japanese Zeroes. Not a single white newspaper picked up the story. I talked to his family, got some pictures and we're doing a full layout."

"I love it. We're going to need a lot more Dorie Miller stories. Now go find them."

Everyone begins to head back to their desks. Ira motions Erma to stay for a minute.

"Are we still on for tonight?"

"Sure. Shall I bring dinner?"

"How about Italian? I'm feeling Rigoletto'ish?"

"What does that feel like?" she laughed.

"Like veal scallopini and a soft Chianti."

"I'll bring the scallopini, you provide the Chianti."

"Ovviamente!"

"Oooh! I love when you talk dirty."

"Back to your letters to the Editor, Weddings and..."

"...bake sales. Arrivederci!"

As Erma returned to her desk she hears "copy" and runs to the voice. It's Paul with the column Ira had asked him to write. They don't say anything to one another, the edginess between them had never gone away. She grabbed his column and walked down the stairs to typesetting. As usual, she reads it before handing it off to Sam. Erma finds herself reading out loud: 'James Thompson, black, 26, was beaten as he waited to enlist at the Army office in downtown Wichita, Kansas. While his injuries were minor it should be noted that the white boys who injured Mr. Thompson kept shouting that 'this is a white man's war.'

I can write better than that, she said to herself. She puts a piece of paper into the typewriter and her fingers danced across the keys. Satisfied, she rereads it quickly and hands it to Sam before returning to her desk.

Chapter Eleven

The next few days Erma stayed home with a bad cold. Maybe it was the winter that was extra cold this year, or a draft in the office. or not enough sleep, but whatever it was, she ached all over. Bessie became like a mother hen, checking on her every few hours, bringing her soup or hot tea.

"Feeling any better, Erma?" she asked.

"Barely. I'm not sure which is running faster, my nose or the other end."

Bessie leaned over and put her hand on Erma's forehead. "Doesn't feel as if you've got a fever."

"After two days in bed, I hope not. I missed a lovely date with my boss and I hope they won't fire me for missing work."

"I brought you today's edition of the *Courier*. Now you relax. I'll come by later with some dinner."

"Thanks, Bessie. You're a dear."

Erma took the paper and began to scan the articles. There it was on page three, Paul's article that she'd rewritten.

'A young patriotic black youth was beaten by a gang of whites simply for trying to serve his country....' Who says I can't write...that is much better than what Paul had written.

The next day she felt well enough to go to work. She'd no sooner taken off her coat and stored her purse in the drawer when Ira motioned her to his office. Paul was already there, his body tense, his arms crossed.

95

"You wanted to see me, Ira? Good morning, Paul"

"We missed you. Are you feeling better?"

"I am. Sorry I missed work."

"We all get sick once in a while. Tell me, why did you rewrite Paul's story?"

"I often do rewrites."

"You correct spelling errors, fix grammar," Paul said, his tone clearly one of controlled rage. "You have no right to completely change a story."

"But..."

"Paul's right. Don't do it again...understood?"

"I'm sorry Paul...Ira. But Paul, your story told the facts but said nothing about the harm to Jimmy Thompson."

"When I want lessons on how to write a story it won't be from a snot-nosed kid. Ira, are we done? I've got work to do."

"We're done," Ira said matter-of-factly.

Paul exited, anger still in his eyes. Erma brushed away a tear.

"Erma, for the record, what you wrote belonged on the Opinion page. You went beyond news reporting when you did more than just report the facts."

"If that's what you want. But when blacks are treated badly, I think we should shout it."

"And as soon as you become Editor you can tell everyone to write that way. But as long as I'm the Editor we're going to do it my way."

Erma returned to her desk. She sat for several minutes trying to calm her emotions. Paul had embarrassed her in front of Ira and worse, Ira had taken his side. Finally, finished with her self-pity but still upset, she grabbed her coat and left the building. There was a small park nearby. She found an empty bench and parked herself there, trying to settle the turmoil in her mind. It wasn't easy to separate emotion from plain criticism. She gave herself twenty minutes, no more. It was something her father had taught her.

You get twenty minutes to take care of whatever is bothering you, then you have to get back to work. She stood, gave her body a good shake and marched herself back to her desk at the *Courier*. The small stack of Letters to the Editor that had been gathering dust were still on her desk, waiting for her. Then, not yet ready, she got herself a cup of coffee, took a deep breath, and grabbed a letter opener. She feigned slitting her throat, resigned herself to reading the letters, and hoping that Ira's upset wasn't too serious, she read the first letter.

"Your newspaper boy keeps throwing my paper in the bushes and..."

She threw the letter into her waste basket and grabbed another.

"Can you please tell someone to stop printing the Obituaries in such a small type size? They're too hard to read."

Convinced this exercise was a complete waste of time, she carefully folded the letter, then balled it up, making a basketball shot into the waste basket. Frustrated, she selected another letter.

"Should I sacrifice my life to live half American? Will things be better for the next generation in the peace to follow? Would it be asking too much to demand full citizenship rights in exchange for the sacrificing of my life? Is the kind of America I know worth defending?"

She stopped reading and looked at the envelope. "Kansas! Wichita, Kansas!"

She read the letter a second time, trying to absorb the words and their meaning. And Wichita, Kansas. Where had she seen that name recently? Oh, my God, Paul's article. The young man who'd been beaten up. He'd written a letter and here it was, a thousand miles away, on my desk. What to do? What to do?

She walked around the office, avoiding eye contact. She didn't want to upset Ira or confront Paul. Maybe she should talk to Wendall, who was sitting at his desk speaking on the telephone. Maybe Frank. No, he'd tell her to show it to Ira. She sat back down and began to reread the letter.

"Let colored Americans adopt the Double V for a double victory - The first V for victory over our enemies without and the second V for our enemies within."

A Double V! Racial equality! She kept repeating the phrases over and over in her head. Finally, she made a decision and marched into Ira's office.

"Ira, we can't have dinner tonight and I need the weekend off."

"If this is about Paul, don't take it so seriously."

"It isn't about Paul."

"Then what is it? A half hour ago we were all set. I was looking forward to you and the scaloppini."

"I'm sorry, something came up."

"Do you mind telling me what earth-shattering event is as important as a good Chianti?"

"Please, Ira. Can I tell you Monday?"

"I'm not sure why you're being so mysterious but, I guess, if it's that important."

"Trust me, Ira. Please trust me, and thank you, thank you, thank you."

Erma leaned over Ira's desk and planted a kiss before rushing back to her desk. Quietly, she picked up the telephone and arranged for a round trip train ticket to Wichita, Kansas, leaving the next morning.

Chapter Twelve

The next morning, while most people were still snuggled in their beds, Erma got herself up, dressed, and to the city's train station. It would be leaving at 7:00 a.m., go to Chicago, where she'd change trains to Wichita. She settled in comfortably when an elderly, colored woman approached.

"Good morning, is this seat taken?"

"No, please sit down," Erma responded.

"Are you going to Chicago?" the woman asked, removing her coat and folding it carefully.

"Yes, and no. I'm actually going to Wichita, that's in Kansas. I'll be changing trains in Chicago."

Friendly and, obviously wanting to chat, the woman continued.

"That's a long train ride. Are you traveling alone? I mean you seem so young...but maybe that's because I'm so old."

Erma smiled. "You aren't that old. My name is Erma, Erma Chandler."

"How do you do? My name is Olympia Overton. I'm visiting my daughter. She and her husband just had my first grandchild, Naomi Watson, 6 pounds, 7 ounces. They're picking me up when I arrive and then we'll drive to Cicero. That's where they live. I'm so excited."

"I can imagine. Grandparents have a very special relationship."

"Definitely. We get to spoil them and leave the rearing to their parents. My only worry now is that my daughter tells me my son-in-law wants to enlist in the Navy. I mean, he's a new father. He'd be leaving my daughter with a new baby. What is it with young men?"

"I don't think they're taking men with young children yet and if he's coloured they may not want him at all," Erma declared.

"I hope not. Do you have family in Wichita?"

"No, I'm going there on business."

"Really. That's very impressive for a woman as young as you...and as pretty."

"You're so sweet. I'm a reporter for a newspaper, the *Pittsburgh Courier*. Do you know it?"

"Oh, yes. My husband, Roger, always read it. Said it reported things white papers ignored. He passed last year."

"I'm sorry."

"We were married for thirty years," Olympia said, sadly.

At that moment the Conductor came by, interrupting their conversation. Olympia Overton eyed him nervously. Once he passed, she resumed speaking, but continued to watch the man until he left the car.

"Conductors make me nervous," she said. "When I was a young girl in Louisiana, we had to ride in separate cars for Negroes. I always think they're going to make me do that. They don't that here up north but I always think about it," she sighed. "Tell me how such a young girl got to be a reporter for a big newspaper."

"I guess I was lucky. I met a young man when I arrived in Pittsburgh and he got me an interview. I had just arrived in the big city from a small-town south of Pittsburgh ...Fayette."

"Fayette? Oh, what a coincidence. My sister lives in Fayette."

"My father is a Preacher there," Erma said.

"Well, I'll write her. I'm sure they know one another. It's such a small town."

The two women continued to chat until the Conductor returned.

"Chicago next stop," he said loudly. "Ten minutes. Chicago, final stop!"

"Excuse me, sir," Erma said as he came by. "I'm connecting to Wichita."

"That'll be Track 16," he said, checking his schedule. "Scheduled to leave at 11:45. You should make it just fine."

"Thank you."

Erma helped the woman walk into the Concourse and said her goodbye as the woman's family approached.

With the time change working in her favor, Erma hoped to be at the Thompson house by mid-afternoon. She'd called and spoken to Jimmy. He sounded very pleasant over the telephone but a little confused about why she was coming.

The train arrived at Wichita's tiny station right on schedule. Erma crossed the platform and exited to the short line of waiting cabs.

"Can you take me to this address?

"That's what I'm here for, lady. $3.50 plus tip."

Erma nodded and got in. 'plus tip' was something she'd never heard and she couldn't help wondering whether it was because the driver was white and she was colored.

They drove through the city, eventually passing Wichita's central area and reaching a poorer, colored neighborhood. The driver stopped and pointed to the small yellow house. It was neatly kept with a small flower bed in front. She paid the driver, plus a tip. He seemed satisfied and drove off.

Jimmy Thompson opened the door. My God, he's so young, Erma thought. He could be my older brother. She saw the bandage on his cheek but he smiled and they were no longer strangers.

In the living room, two people waited, Clyde Thompson, Jimmy's father, and a young girl, Jimmy's girlfriend, Annie Culver. Clyde had distinguished grey hair. He was wearing an old cardigan sweater and Erma knew he'd had that sweater a long time. It was more than a sweater. It was memories and holes or no holes, you don't discard memories. Annie had that young, adorable, scrubbed look. She and Jimmy made a very handsome couple.

Clyde and Annie greeted Erma warmly as they moved to the small living room with its old furniture, worn arms covered with lace doilies.

"Can I get you some coffee, Erma?" Annie asked.

"No, thank you. I had two cups in Chicago changing trains. My, that is a huge terminal. Much larger than what we have in Pittsburgh"

"Or Wichita," Clyde added.

"Or Wichita," Erma agreed, nervous that her inexperience was showing.

"Miss Chandler...Erma, what makes a big city newspaper like the *Courier* interested in a letter my boy wrote?" Clyde asked.

"Mr. Thompson, I read all the Letters to the Editor that come into us. Most are just people letting off steam about one thing or another. Jimmy's letter was different."

"Different how?" Annie asked.

Erma felt herself become calmer and more confident. These people could have been her kin. They were warm and welcoming to strangers.

"His letter spoke to the frustrations of more than twelve million Negroes in a way I had never heard before. It said our country is at war and I want to help but I want that help to mean something. If we're going to shed our blood the same as white soldiers, we'd like to return home as equals."

Annie and Clyde knew about Jimmy's letter. Annie had even corrected some of Jimmy's spelling and grammar but listening to Erma somehow put the letter into an entirely different context.

"And that's what brought you here?" Jimmy asked.

"I wanted to know more about the young man who wrote the letter and what prompted him to send it to us"

Clyde looked at his son. "I'm not sure, either. Jimmy?"

Jimmy started to speak, stopped, grabbed Annie's hand nervously, and started again.

"I should probably explain some of what was goin' on those few weeks before that letter was written."

"Tell it anyway that makes sense to you," Erma said, urging him with a supportive smile.

"The whole town was shocked when our country got attacked. And when President Roosevelt declared war against the Japs and Germans, everyone in Wichita cheered. There were parades and it seemed like everyone was flag waving. The folks at the Cessna factory... that's where we all work, called us together to tell us we'd be building lots of airplanes for the Air Corps. We all felt sort'a together, patriotic. It was a real good feeling.

"The local papers had pictures of young men waiting in lines to enlist. In the center of town there were tables set up by Army recruiters. I told Annie that I was gon'na enlist. It was a Wednesday. I went down to the Recruiting place. I was excited to enlist, and…"

Jimmy's voice broke and he stopped talking, remembering that day, he wiped away a tear.

"Several young men, all white, had gathered outside the Recruiting office, waiting for it to open. As I approached, I could hear their conversation. Just a bunch of guys B.S.-ing. When they saw me, they stopped and watched as I approached.

"Their comments were less than friendly but this was an Army enlistment office I was going to. I felt pretty safe and I answered that I'd come to enlist. Was this the line, I asked? I didn't expect the reaction I got.

"Enlist?" they asked. "You must be bat-shit crazy. Go home! This is a white man's war."

"They all began crowding around me. The one with the baseball jacket knocked me down and they all began kicking me, laughing and calling me names. I tried to protect myself. After a few minutes, the Recruiting door opened and they walked away. The Army guy told me to go home. No blacks wanted. I picked myself up slowly and headed home."

Erma's pencil hung over her notepad and her hand trembled at the sadness in Jimmy's voice. He took a sip of water and continued.

"I never really knew Wichita to be like that. I guess I was pretty naïve. I mean, you might hear about things like that happening in Mississippi or Alabama, but not Kansas. Wow, did I grow up in a hurry."

"What happened after that?" Erma asked.

"That was another revelation. The Recruiting Sergeant came out to separate us but totally ignored me. When I got home, I was confused and angry. I just sat in the dark, trying to make sense of what had happened."

Silence hung in the room before Clyde patted his son on the shoulder.

"I saw Jimmy's bruises and the sadness in his eyes that evening. I didn't know what had happened, but I knew it wasn't good. I didn't say anything, just sat there, quiet, waiting until he was ready to speak. When he finally explained, tears welled up inside me. I'd worked so hard all these years to shield him and now the hatred in the world had broken through."

"My parents raised me to be proud of being an American," Jimmy interjected. "We hung our flag every July 4th and we visited the Old Soldier's home every Armistice Day. But now my Dad was telling me things I'd never heard him say before."

"Like what?" Erma asked.

"Like the real reason we'd moved from Omaha when Jimmy was young," Clyde said, walking across the room and sitting down next to Erma.

"I'd always believed it was just the Depression," Jimmy said. "My Dad told us he'd been offered a better job and maybe a better life here in Wichita."

"That was a part of it. The part I'd never talked about was that the Hormel meat factory where I worked was planning a big layoff. The white workers had gotten together and told the Managers that if any 'colored' kept a job with a white being laid off, they'd torch the factory and kill all the 'darkies.'"

"Would Hormel do that? Keep Negroes and lay off whites," Erma asked, now writing furiously.

"The whites were all in the Union. Got paid more. It was the Depression. Management needed to keep labor costs down. The Union didn't accept coloreds and we all got paid less...a lot less."

"I guess leaving Omaha made sense and with a job waiting in Wichita..."

Clyde continued, a sadness in his voice. "I always knew there were two Americas...a white America and a colored America, with bad schools, biased police, and too much poverty. And even if you worked hard, you couldn't always shield your family from a lot of the ugliness."

"This was my first experience with real racism," Jimmy said, grabbing Annie's hand and handing her a tissue to dry her tears. "What I'd learned about Abe Lincoln and the Emancipation Proclamation and all those Amendments were just pieces of paper. A big part of the country just ignores 'em when it comes to livin' their lives. It all set me thinkin.' It was wrong. There shouldn't be two Americas and if we're gon'na be fightin' a war we ought'a be able to see a better America when it's over. I tried to put it all down on paper. I'd write something, tear it up, and start again. It finally said what I wanted it to."

"Well, you expressed it beautifully. You really did. What are your plans now?"

"I still want to get into the war."

"I wanted him to finish college first. Maybe we'd get married," Annie said through glazed eyes.

"And I might have gotten him transferred to be a Mechanic's apprentice," Clyde added. "But Jimmy is stubborn. His mother, bless her soul, was the same way."

He moved to the mantle and carefully picked up a framed photograph. Lovingly, he showed it to Erma.

"That's Rosemary, Jimmy's mother, and me, right after Jimmy was born."

"I can see the love in the photo. What happened?"

"Three years after Jimmy was born, she died in childbirth. The only black doctor for miles was sick. White doctor wouldn't treat her, white hospital wouldn't admit her."

Erma blanched, "I'm so sorry."

She watched as Clyde kissed the photograph and returned it to the mantle. What was there to say. She was an intruder and these people had opened their deepest feelings. Jimmy finally broke the silence.

"Erma, is there any way you or the *Courier* can help get me into this war?"

"I don't know, Jimmy, but I'll look into it and let you know. Meanwhile, with your permission I want to see if I can convince our paper to reprint your Double V thoughts."

"Sure. That would be great."

"Are you returning to Pittsburgh today?" Clyde asked.

"I am, but I have a little time. Any chance I can see the factory where you work? I've never seen how they build airplanes."

"Sure. Now that we're building more planes, we even have a crew working Saturdays."

Chapter Thirteen

Wichita was a small town, nothing was very far, and the factory was on the outskirts, a short drive. As Erma looked up, she could see a small airplane circling. Inside the factory, despite the loud noise of engines being tested, it was all business. Overhead cranes moved large partially assembled planes while men on the factory floor, mostly white, all wearing coveralls, welded or assembled along a moving line.

"Most of our airplanes use Lycoming engines. Our AT-17 Bobcat twin engine is what we do best. We've been producing five planes each month but we're told they want to double that."

"It's all very impressive and you sound pretty knowledgeable."

"My dad is the knowledgeable one. He has a real important job. He keeps all the machines working. He's one of the best mechanics they've got. I was just working here part-time while I was taking night classes at college."

Across the factory floor two men chatted when they spotted Jimmy and Erma. One was Charlie Simpson, a Supervisor. He was with an overweight older man Jimmy didn't know. Charlie was in his late '20's, brusque with red hair and a temper that always made Jimmy try to avoid him.

They stopped their conversation and, not smiling, approached Jimmy and Erma.

"Hey, what're you people doing here?" Charlie demanded.

"Charlie, it's me Jimmy. Clyde's son."

"I know who you are, kid. But what are you doing here and who is this woman?"

"This is Erma Chandler. She's a reporter from the *Pittsburgh Courier*. She came to Wichita to talk about a letter I wrote. She asked if she could see the factory. She had a couple of hours before her train. I didn't think it would be a problem. Erma, this is Charlie Simpson, one of the factory foremen."

"How do you do, Charlie. Impressive factory you have here."

Charlie stared at Erma, dislike in his eyes, sarcasm in his voice. "Kid, I didn't even know you can write. Now, listen up. This factory is making airplanes for the Army. It isn't a damned tourist attraction. Neither of you belong here. This isn't your shift and if she really is a reporter, and I ain't ever seen a colored reporter, much less a female, she needs approval from the front office. You got that approval, whatever your name is?"

"Erma Chandler, and if you'll point me in the right direction, I'll take care of getting the necessary approvals."

"Not today you won't. It's Saturday. They don't work on Saturday." Charlie's friend added, making it clear he felt the same as Charlie. These coloreds shouldn't be here.

"So, you lovely people, move your collective brown behinds out of here."

"There's no reason to be nasty, Charlie. Miss Chandler has come a long way. We're not harming anyone."

"Sez who? I see 'niggers' where they don't belong and, bein' of a suspicious nature, I want to know what they're up to.

112

Until the war started this factory was mostly whites. Now coloreds comin' in takin' some of those good payin' jobs."

"Ain't right." Charlie's friend added.

"As I said, you are where you don't belong. We got a plant to run, and airplanes to build, so we can win a war and make things safe for all the folks. Even all the coons!"

Erma's bile was rising. In a different environment she might have lost her temper, but this wasn't the time or place. Instead, she feigned charm. "Why, thank you, Charlie. I'm sure our readers will be grateful to know how solicitous you are of our safety."

"Huh?" was all Charlie could muster.

"Before I leave, I want to make sure I've got your names correctly. You're Charlie Simpson, right?"

"Right."

"And what's your name?"

The other man looked confused before stammering an answer, "Peter Strump."

"Strump? Really?"

"Yeah. You got a problem with that?"

"Oh, no. It's such a...". She paused to keep herself from laughing. "It's such a refined name."

"Why you want my name?"

"For my story. And Dwane Wallace, he's the President of Cessna, right?"

"Yeah. He and his brother, Dwight, run the company."

"And they pretty much rely on Army contracts?"

"Why you asking all these questions? You need to leave."

"We'll leave, but you need to know my boss, Ira Lewis, is on a first name basis with the Secretary of War who runs the Army and gives out the contracts that keep this place humming and gives you your job. One call and Mr. Wallace

113

will get an earful about how we've been treated. Now you all have a nice day. C'mon, Jimmy, I've seen enough."

Erma turned to leave. Jimmy suppressed a smile as Charlie and Pete stood, frozen and left to wonder and worry.

"Does your boss really know the Secretary of War?" Jimmy asked.

"No, but those red necks don't know that."

Chapter Fourteen

Monday morning Erma had come to the office early but Ira was already there, grumpy.

"Good morning, Erma. Did you have a good weekend?"

"I did, thank you."

"I had to go to a movie...alone. I saw the Ghost of Frankenstein."

"Oooh. A scary movie. Weren't you afraid?"

"Lon Chaney played the monster. He wasn't as scary as Boris Karloff."

"I'm sure you handled it beautifully."

"So, are you going to tell me why you canceled our date... and my scallopini?"

"I went to Wichita."

"Wichita? In Kansas?"

"Yes. That Wichita."

"Why?"

"I think I've uncovered a terrific story."

"You went to Kansas to get a story? You couldn't find anything to write about in Pittsburgh?"

"I could but this was special. Here, read this Letter to the Editor that came in last week."

Ira took the letter reluctantly and began to read aloud.

"Will America be a true and pure democracy after this war? Will colored Americans still suffer the indignities that have been heaped upon them in the past?"

Ira stopped reading and tried to hand the letter back to Erma.

"Is this from the same kid that spawned the issue with Paul?"

"It is. After being beaten up, the boy wrote us a Letter to the Editor. Now, please, keep reading."

Ira looked at her. He had important things to do but Erma's glare was intense and at the moment he didn't want to upset her. He continued reading.

"I suggest that while we keep victory in the forefront, we don't lose sight of our fight for true democracy at home. The "V for Victory" sign is being displayed for victory over aggression, slavery and tyranny. Then let colored Americans adopt the Double V for a double victory."

Suddenly Erma's voice joined his.

"Colored Americans will come into their own, and America will eventually become the true democracy it was designed to be. I'm willing to die for the America I know will someday become a reality"

"You memorized it?"

"Part of it. I read and reread it on the train to and from Wichita. It sent shivers up my spine, Ira, it really did. It's powerful, and a hell'uva story. Picture it. A frustrated colored boy, unwilling to accept the world as he finds it imagines a better world. A world in which all races are equal. A V for Victory in the war and a V for racial equality at home. A Double V!"

"A wonderful concept, like Motherhood and Apple Pie, God and Country. Now, please leave me. I have work to do running a newspaper."

"But, Ira, don't you see what we can do with it to get blacks into this war? A Double V! Win the war and eliminate racism."

"OK, it's pretty extreme but if you want to do an Op-Ed piece, I'll look at it."

Erma returned to her desk and pulled out her notes. She got herself comfortable and started typing, and deleting, and typing some more. When she finished, she took her column into Ira's office. She waited quietly while he finished a phone call. Ira read it, red penciled some lines, added another, and smiled as he returned it to her.

"You're actually starting to write like a reporter."

"I still think it belongs on page one as a news story."

"Of course, you do," Ira smiled. "And in big bold type. It's an Op-Ed! Be grateful!"

"Yes, sir," she said sheepishly.

"We're not going to do much until we see what the public thinks. Get the Art Department to come up with a logo. Maybe add an eagle or something patriotic."

"Do I get a byline for finding the story?"

"It's an Op-Ed. I guess a byline is OK."

"Imagine, me, Erma Chandler, I'm finally getting my name on an important story."

"It isn't important...yet. At this point it's on the Opinion page."

"You'll see. It will be news!"

"And, please, tell me next time before you run off. I hate going to the movies alone."

As Erma started to leave, she reached out to thank Ira but he didn't let go, instead pulling her close and kissing her passionately.

"And don't forget you still have Church socials to write about," he said softly.

"And bake sales. I know."

Reaction to the article was swift. Within days Ira had received calls from white and black newspaper Editors around the country, many asking if they could reprint Jimmy's letter, lauding the idea of the Double V. Ira was surprised, Erma wasn't.

A few mornings later he gathered the news staff.

"Hey, everyone," Ira said loudly. "Please stop what you're doing for a few minutes."

"Ira, we've got a deadline coming up," Frank Bolden objected. "I want to finish this column."

"I know. I'll only take a moment. Guys, I want to light a fuse in the country and I want the *Courier* holding the match."

"I use a lighter myself," Tom kidded. "So much more sophisticated."

Ira glowered, not happy. "Can the humor! This is serious. The Japanese are kicking our asses across the Pacific. Hitler is about to invade England and Negroes in the U.S. are mostly sitting on the sidelines. It isn't right. Erma uncovered something and I've decided the *Courier* is going to run with it."

Erma stepped forward, exuding a newfound confidence.

"We represent a lot of people who don't have a voice. Coloreds need to be in there, fighting side by side with white boys. We want to be there. This war can be a real leap forward. Shedding our blood alongside white soldiers earns us the right to demand equality. It's a chance to prove that the American Negro is as patriotic as a white American and just as interested in winning this war."

"I read your Op-Ed," Paul interrupted, "And, frankly, I wasn't happy that the story I initially reported on had been co-opted by an inexperienced wannabe. But, aside from that, you're preaching to the choir. We all want to get our people out of the unskilled jobs and into management."

"Even the few coloreds in the service are either below deck on ships or cleaning latrines," Wendall chimed in. "I mean, what would our brave white fighting men do without them clean bathrooms?"

"Save your humor for the comics," Ira said. "Anyway, we're gon'na try it out...see if it resonates. We're starting a Double V campaign. A V for victory in the war and a V for victory in racial equality at home."

"Ira, with all due respect, that isn't reporting news, it's making news," Frank insisted. "That isn't what newspapers do. You tested it on the Op-Ed page. Why not keep it there? You start getting pushy on race issues, you're gon'na offend your white advertisers. I've seen it happen before. The *Courier* could take a real hit, financially."

"Until Pearl Harbor I'd agree with you but this war has changed everything. Right now, it's a white man's war."

"We need to stir things up," Erma interrupted.

"We'll just have to hope our advertisers hang in there with us."

"Let me be sure I understand," Frank asked. "You want us to tell our colored readers to be more conscious of being treated unfairly rather than supporting the war effort?"

"No, Frank," Erma said defensively, standing to make her point. "We want all of America to understand that Negro boys are as willing to die in defense of their country as white boys and shouldn't be excluded because of their skin color."

Ira found himself getting more and more enthusiastic about the Double V.

"Six months ago, Roosevelt signed an Executive Order prohibiting racial exclusion in defense jobs and housing. It was a first step but most of the country has ignored it. I'm hoping this Double V idea will take it further and energize coloreds and fair thinking whites. Anyway, we're going to try it. When you can, bend your stories to include it."

"You're the boss."

"Damn right! Ok, everyone back to work. Erma, can I see you for a minute in my office?"

Erma followed Ira into his office, exhilarated by the launching of the Double V.

"Erma, you look especially attractive today."

"That's because it's a special day."

"Special? How?"

"Lots'a reasons. The Double V. I'm sure we're doing the right thing...and it's the six- month anniversary of our first date."

"Oh! Well, that wasn't really a date."

"You kissed me. That made it a date."

"That kiss was just a social nicety."

"Uh-huh! You say tomato, I say to-mat-o."

"I'll show you," Ira took Erma in his arms and kissed her. Any resistance melted away.

"Was that 'tomato' or 'to-mat-o'?"

"I'll let you decide. Now, when can we do scaloppini and chianti? I have the Chianti anxiously awaiting your arrival."

"And can we talk about our future? I'm not getting any younger."

Ira broke out laughing. "Are you kidding? You couldn't BE any younger. Erma, I'm too old for you. I love our time together but I've been married and divorced. Marriage has left me scarred."

"Uh-huh! You've sung that song before. I know all the lyrics."

"Yes, they're catchy. I was thinking of asking Louie Armstrong to record them for us."

"I'd make you the perfect Betty Crocker wife. Dinner on the table, your underpants ironed."

"Erma, you're a working reporter. And you're becoming a damned good one. You aren't cut out to be a stay-at-home wife."

"If I remember correctly, your first wife was a stay-at-home wife early in your marriage. How'd that work out?"

"Not too well, but that's beside the point."

"So, what's the point?"

"My scaloppini. When are we having dinner?"

"Tonight."

"Yum!"

"Yum yourself. This subject isn't over."

Chapter Fifteen

J. Edgar Hoover was appointed the head of what would become the F.B.I. as far back as 1924. Since then, it had evolved to become America's elite crime-fighting organization. Along with his autocratic supervision, he had built dossiers on everyone in the country of any importance. His position as Chief had become unassailable.

The day after the attack on Pearl Harbor, President Franklin D. Roosevelt gave the FBI emergency authority to censor all news and control all communications in and out of the country. The Alien Act, passed the year before, already prohibited advocating or teaching the "propriety of over-throwing or destroying any government in the United States by force or violence" and the printing or publishing of any material advocating or teaching the violent overthrow of the country. Winning the war was the nation's singular objective. The country was threatened, efforts to combat racism were irrelevant.

And now some damn newspaper in Pittsburgh wasn't playing ball, stirring up feelings of racial discontent. He would not countenance it. Hoover had called William Taylor, one of his agents into his office. He was going to nip this crap in the bud."

"Bill, are you aware of this subversive Negro campaign that seems to be gaining traction?"

"No, sir."

"You should be. What have you been working on?"

"German infiltration of our defense plants."

"Oh, right. Let Campbell handle that. This is a new problem and it needs some delicacy. We don't want to get the coloreds riled up."

"Yes, sir. I mean, no, sir."

"I'm sending what information we have to your desk as we speak. It isn't much, mostly newspaper articles. The *Pittsburgh Courier* seems to be taking the lead on a campaign called The Double V, whatever the crap that means."

"Yes, sir."

"Stop saying 'yes, sir', 'no, sir' will you for Christ's sakes?"

"Yes, sir. Oh, sorry."

"The *Courier* wants the full participation of 'niggers' in the war, Army, Navy, the whole shebang. Most of the Generals and Admirals don't want the problems that would come with having to deal with it. They have a war to fight that our country wasn't prepared for. We, that is, the United States government, want everyone focusing on the war, not race issues. You understand that."

"I do."

"Good, now get out of here and fix the problem."

"Yes, sir.... I mean, I will, Mr. Hoover."

Chapter Sixteen

Ira entered the newsroom, his shoulders bent, his brow furrowed. Frank Bolden was already there, typing his next column.

"Why so glum? You walk as if you've got the entire world on your shoulders."

"The war news. Japs bayoneting children in China. Jews being rounded up across Europe and Russia's 2^d largest city, Leningrad, blockaded by the Germans."

"I know. It's terrible."

"It feels like we're fighting the Devil Incarnate. I spoke with Senator Guffey. He's still on the sidelines when I ask about more Negro participation. What are you working on so intently?"

"Detroit! The Sojourner Housing Project. Remember the Government approved building houses to ease the shortage of homes for all the new factory workers. Well, the shortages had hit everyone and now blacks and whites are beating the crap out of one another, each one claiming the other got preferential treatment. Look at these photos. Europe isn't the only place these days that are violent. Several people dead, dozens injured."

As Frank was showing the photos to Ira, Erma rushed in, throwing off her coat, and spreading a stack of newspapers on Ira's desk.

"Sure, barge in," Ira said, irritated. "Do you care what Frank and I were discussing. No, you do not."

"You're right. I'm sorry, but look, we're being flooded with letters supporting the Double V. And other papers around the country are starting to promote the idea. Five Congressmen have also spoken in support of it on the floor of the House."

"OK, your rudeness is forgiven, for now, but at least it's something positive. We have our 'hook.' I want every story to mention the Double V campaign, racial equality, Negro participation in the war. Get celebrities …athletes…politicians on board. And get me photographs! Lots of photographs. Hallelujah!" Ira said, elated, rubbing his hands together.

"OK, Ira. You've succeeded in getting attention. Probably even increasing circulation…"

"It will definitely increase circulation AND ad revenue. Don't forget that. Advertising revenue is 'mother's milk.' Pays all our salaries."

"Maybe, but it's also going to generate a really mean backlash."

"You mean some white folks are going to get upset?"

"Don't sound so cavalier. It could be a lot more than that. The big national newspapers, like the New York Times, ran an Editorial yesterday. They think we're diverting too much attention away from the war. Some politicians are saying we should be investigated for helping the enemy by stirring up colored folks. There are laws against that during wartime."

"They want us to continue sitting on our asses," Erma said angrily.

"I won't do it, Frank," said Ira decisively. "I've just just reached the limit of what I'm willing to tolerate and sitting in the back of the bus isn't one of them. If we're going to stir up colored folks and liberals to get action, then that's what we'll do.

"Now we're going to lend our voice to the demand for 'proportional representation.' I'm writing an Op-Ed for tomorrow's paper. Double V, proportional representation. That's our mantra. Double V is the goal. Proportional representation is the first step toward that goal."

"Proportional representation?" Erma repeated. "The average 'Joe' on the street can't pronounce 'proportional representation,' much less understand it."

"Then you and the others are lousy reporters. Explain it to them. If the country is going to enlist 100 white soldiers, it

127

will also enlist 10 colored soldiers because we're 10% of the population, AND..."

"...If there are 100 jobs at a factory or 100 new 'whatever's being offered....

"...Negroes get 10. Got it!" Erma smiled.

Frank added his slant. "A fair share of the American dream."

Their enthusiasm became infectious. Erma stood, waving her hands. "We'll caption our stories 'the true American spirit.' We can start a photo series... 'From the rock-bound coast of Maine to San Francisco's Golden Gate, the Double V is igniting the nation.'"

"And, Erma...put it into all your Church stories. We want to hear about the Double V in every sermon from every pulpit."

Erma laughs at the idea. "Got it! Jesus supports the Double V."

"See if you can a direct quote from him, and Frank, watch your ass. They're going to come for us. "

Chapter Seventeen

Senator Joseph Guffey, the Junior Senator from Pennsylvania was in his office working when he got a visit from William Taylor of the FBI. Guffey had ridden the wave of Franklin Roosevelt's popularity in 1932 and won reelection again in 1938. He was a heavyset, cigar-smoking, very savvy politician who endeared himself to white majorities and black minorities, to farmers and office clerks, men and women.

He greeted Taylor as if the FBI agent were an old member of his family.

"Mr. Taylor. Come in, come in. I don't often get visits from the FBI. Please, sit down! I was impressed with Mr. Hoover's testimony last year in front of our Senate Committee. Now, what can I do for you? I haven't broken any Federal laws that I know of," he laughed in a manner of two long-time friends and drinking buddies.

Bill Taylor had been in the FBI for nearly a decade. He was long immune to flattery from Congressional members, nervous about what might be in Mr. Hoover's dossier file.

"No, sir, this is a collegial call. I met with Mr. Hoover yesterday. He asked me to send his salutations. We've been looking into a situation that was brewing and he thought you might be able to help us with it."

"Certainly, if I can. I have great respect for Mr. Hoover and the work the FBI is doing on behalf of our nation.

Especially now, during war time, rooting out fascist sympathizers."

"The FBI is very grateful for your support."

"Would you like some coffee...or, perhaps, something stronger? A cigar?"

"No, I'm fine. As I'm sure you'll agree, this is a particularly difficult time in our country, moving out of a depression and a peacetime economy to a wartime footing. We must have the entire country focused on defeating the enemy."

"Absolutely! And, I want to assure you, the Commonwealth of Pennsylvania, that I am blessed to represent, is doing its share. Our coal, steel, and aluminum factories are working overtime to produce the war materiel our military boys need."

"Of course, but the issue that concerns me...and Mr. Hoover, is the colored population."

"The Negroes? Oh, I'm sure they're doing their patriotic role."

"The *Pittsburgh Courier* recently launched something called the Double V campaign, a V for victory in the war and a V for racial equality at home."

"And?"

"As long as that campaign stayed in Pittsburgh it wasn't a problem but we think it's beginning to gain national traction and that it will distract attention from the war. We don't want to deal with racism during war time."

"Certainly not."

"We were hoping you'd speak with the Publisher of the *Courier*, convince him to stop this campaign."

"Ira Lewis! I know him well. I'm happy to call him. Ira is a good man. I'm sure it won't be a problem."

"Thank you, Senator. I'll let Mr. Hoover know we have your support."

"God bless Mr. Hoover and the FBI. Good day, sir."

Once Bill Taylor left, the Senator took a deep breath and poured himself a drink. That went well, he thought. Those people are scary, all dressed alike in dark suits and their wing-tip shoes. You never know what they're thinking. He warmed himself with a long sip of his bourbon and shouted to his secretary, "Flo, get Ira Lewis of the *Pittsburgh Courier* on the phone, please."

Ira Lewis was in his office when the telephone rang. It was a rare day in Pittsburgh thanks to winds that cleared the skies and the perpetual smells. The sun reflected off the rivers. It was definitely a good day to be alive. He picked up the phone hoping that nothing would spoil the day. Once he heard the Senator's voice, most of that hope dissipated.

"Ira Lewis here. Senator Guffey. Nice to hear from you. How are things down in Washington?"

"They're fine, Ira. We're all working together to build a military than can win this war quickly. First time in my memory that both parties are cooperating. Now, what is this Double V campaign I'm hearing about?"

"I'm impressed that the Double V has reached the Capitol. Good! It began with a Letter to the Editor we received. A young Negro lad tried to enlist in the Army and was beaten up by some boys shouting that this was a white man's war. The letter he wrote suggested we adopt a Double V."

"Yes, I was told what the Double V represented but, Ira, it's causing a problem."

"Problem? What sort of a problem?"

"I just had a visit from an FBI agent, a Mr. William Taylor. Hoover sent him to see me. Hoover and his minions are claiming that any discussion of racism detracts from the focus on the war and that's a definite no-no these days."

"Hoover? J. Edgar Hoover? Really!"

"He feels that discussions of race at this time are un-American."

"Well, they aren't un-American. And as for diverting attention from the war? That was never our intent. We just want Negroes to be participants in this war and not bystanders."

"But Negroes are involved. How about those Tuskegee pilots?"

"Those Tuskegee pilots? They're nothing more than a token squadron of colored boys flying out-of-date airplanes. The liberals eat it up, but it's more flash than substance. And they're only a small trickle of men. What about the rest of the twelve million of us? We want all of our people full invested in this war."

"Ira..."

"You're a Senator, for Christ's sakes. Can't you make it happen?"

The Senator took another drink. This call wasn't going the way he had promised Bill Taylor, which meant Hoover wouldn't be very happy either.

"I try, Ira. I do. But there is a huge resistance from the Southern states. They shake their fists and raise hell every time anyone mentions arming Negroes."

"Of course, there's resistance. There always is, but let's be serious. You're up for election soon and if you want the support of Pennsylvania's large Negro population, we need to see some progress on this subject."

"Ira, that's not fair. You know I've always supported the Negro people."

"Senator, talk alone won't get it done. Get us proportional representation. It'll get Negroes into the war. And tell the President if he wants the support of the colored people in this country...most of whom voted for him in the past three elections, he needs to get us a chance to fight and prove our patriotism."

"I'll continue the battle, Ira. I will, but I need you to stop writing all these Double V articles.

"We'll consider it, Senator, but get us into the war. That's all we ask. Thank you for calling."

Senator Guffey hung up the phone, and shouted, "God damn it, that man is one intransigent colored son of a bitch."

Five hundred miles to the northwest, Erma entered Ira's office as Ira slammed down his phone and shouted, "God damn it, that man is a hypocritical liberal plain lying son-of-a-bitch."

"Who are you railing about?"

"Our beloved Senator Guffey. I have to be nice to him and he has to be nice to me but I've always wondered what he really feels. When I get off the phone I feel as if I need to take a shower."

"Guffey's a politician. You'll never figure out where he stands."

"You're too young to be cynical."

"Comes from spending too much time with you and Frank."

"Actually, Guffey and I play nice. He needs the Negro vote to get elected. He's a Democrat in a state that can flip either way. And his support has been useful in getting our people better jobs and schools around the state. But enough about him. Are you and I having dinner tonight?"

"Do I have to wear my Double V dress?"

"Only if you agree to take it off later in the evening."

"Then I'll wear something more...accessible. Can we talk about 'us' tonight?"

"'Us?' As in you and I?"

"Yes! As in Lois Lane, star reporter, wants to co-mingle with Clark Kent, A-K-A Superman, boy and girl, birds and bees."

"Erma, you know I love you. But I like my life just the way it is."

"Lonely evenings? Wouldn't it be better to be ka-noodling with Lois Lane, wearing your blue and red cape? Doesn't that sound 'yummy'?"

"Yummy?"

"Sometimes it takes a second try to see how good a marriage can be with the right person. C'mon, jump in the pool, the temperature is perfect."

"We already have a good relationship, and capes don't look good on me. Besides, I still think I'm too old for you."

"Age is only a number. Spiritually we connect."

"Why do we need to get married?"

"To have children and carry our gene pool forward. Wouldn't you like to bounce a little Ira or Madge on your knee?"

"Actually, I'd prefer to bounce their mother on my knee. Besides, I always think of wives keeping the home fires burning, not standing next to me igniting more of them. Let's just stay the way we are."

"It's not enough. You and I can do both. Run the *Pittsburgh Courier* 'til this war ends and then raise a family in peacetime.

I'm a grown woman, educated, AND an accomplished reporter. I can also be a loving wife and a caring mother."

"Great...! I'm in love with Wonder Woman. You're probably even hiding your magic bracelets. I admit I underrated your ability...and your tenacity."

"Tenaciousness is one of my more subtle qualities."

"Oh, yeah. Subtle like a cobra."

"But so much nicer to snuggle with."

"You need to find someone younger and less jaded."

"But we love one another...and you are attracted to me."

"Get back to work...and while you're at it, get me a hot cup of coffee!"

"Your wife would be happy to get you a fresh cup, but your star reporter says...'Get your own damn coffee.'"

Erma started to leave as she ran into Wendall and Frank storming through the door, distressed looks on their faces.

"Ira, the Japs just bombed Darwin in the north of Australia," Wendall cried.

"And the Army has 24,000 troops trapped on the Bataan peninsula. The Japanese are closing in," Frank shouted.

Ira jumped to his feet, sensing the same urgency as his reporters. "Bataan? Where is Bataan, for Christ' sakes?"

"It's one of the islands in the Philippines," Erma added.

"Jesus. if we lose the Philippines, we could easily lose the Hawaiian Islands. Erma, tell them to hold the lead story of today's edition. Wendall, pull everything you've got off the teletype wire and insert the new war bulletins. Stress the seriousness of the situation."

Chapter Eighteen

Jimmy and Clyde were on their afternoon break, enjoying a cup of coffee and looking at the newspaper.

"The war news is terrible," Clyde commented. "Especially in the Pacific. I wonder how long it'll be before we stop 'em. I mean, it looks as if the Philippines are gone."

"Nothing good going on in Europe either. Germans moving at will. Say, pop, did you see that some other papers have printed my letter? Miss Chandler sent me copies."

"It's a real good letter, Jimmy, I told you that before and I'm real proud of you for writing it, but I'm not sure having them include your name in the newspaper is a good thing."

"Why not?"

"It might cause problems. I don't say it will, but it could."

"What kind of problems?"

"Some folks might think that letter sounds uppity... Colored folks demandin' things that ain't never gon'na happen."

"They have to happen sometime, don't they?"

"Black people been sayin' that kinda' shit for near a hundred years. Jimmy, I been a believer most of my life and, I suspect we'll all be sayin' it long after I've gone to the hereafter. But the more time passes, the more I fret you and your children will be hoping the same thing a hundred years from today."

Their conversation was interrupted by an obviously irritated Charlie.

"What're you two jabborin' about? Your break time ended ten minutes ago. This is work time. We've got airplanes to build and people to feed. And Thompson, I want to talk to you."

"Which Thompson?" Clyde asked.

"Your son, the smart-ass one. But you should stay, hear what your damn kid did. He convinced that newspaper lady who was here that day to go ahead and print your letter in their big city newspaper and now it's raising all kinds of hell."

"It was just a letter and that newspaper is a thousand miles away," Clyde said, folding his newspaper and putting the empty coffee cup in the trash.

"Maybe, but it sure traveled faster than any airplane. My boss, and his boss, called me in to find out what's going on. Our company President, Dwayne Wallace himself, got a phone call from the head of the FBI, the Federal Bureau of Investigation in Washington, Mr. J. Edgar Hoover, asking about your letter."

"My letter? How'd he know...?"

"He's the FBI! They know everything."

"Am I in trouble?'

"If it was up to me, I'd fire your ass but, no, you aren't in trouble, at the moment, assuming you ain't writin' any more letters. You got a copy of that letter with you?"

"Here," Jimmy said with a mixture of pride and apprehension. "You can keep it. I've got several."

Charlie grabbed the newspaper and, still scowling, began to scan the article.

"It was that damned colored reporter. She was a real bitch. Double V? Ain't a Double V just a 'W'?"

"Not Jimmy's. His is a new idea...somethin' really special."

138

Charlie's irritation built as he stopped reading and crumbled the newspaper in anger.

"It ain't special, and you ain't special neither," he said, getting up in Jimmy's face.

"Getting people stirred up ain't your place. You're a piss-ant kid. You want equal rights, boy? You think you're as good as white folks?"

"Probably not a good time or place for this conversation, Charlie. Like you said, we need to get back to work."

"We got another minute. So, answer me this, Mr. smart-ass coon kitchen cleaner. You think you're as good as our boss, Mr. Wallace? You as good as him? You better than me? Is that what you're saying. Cause you ain't."

Charlie's voice was hot, his mood threatening.

"You were born colored and that's somethin' that ain't never gon'na change. You, and your kin over in dark Africa, ain't never gon'na be the equal of God-fearin' white folks. So, nigger. you know what you can do with that article in your colored brown paper?"

"There's no reason to talk to the boy that way, Charlie," Clyde pleaded.

"My name is Mr. Simpson. I've allowed you to get familiar and this is what I get. Clyde, you're supposed to fix machines. Get fix'n.'! You don't belong here."

"Charlie...Mr. Simpson..."

"Move! And you, you dishwasher, letter write'n smart ass. You belong in the kitchen. DOUBLE V! Screw your DOUBLE V!"

Chapter Nineteen

Ira was working at his desk when Paul entered without knocking, something that Ira had always found irritating.

"You do understand the function of a door, don't you, Paul?"

"There's been a racial killing."

"Sad as it is, there are always racial killings."

"This one is different. A black kid from New Jersey gets into the Army. They send him to Mississippi for Basic Training. After a couple of weeks, all the recruits got a pass to go into town. He gets on a bus. The white driver tells him to get to the back of the bus. When the kid hesitates, the driver pulls out a gun and shoots him."

"Holy Mother of God! The Army have any comment? The local police? Anyone?"

"I tried. His family is outraged but neither the Army nor the city officials will comment. And, the white press isn't reporting the story. Seems they all got telephone calls telling them to leave it alone, that reporting it could incite race riots."

"Well, that's bullshit. It's a story that needs to be told. Give it some space on the front page. See if the family can provide a picture, and make sure you give the story the outrage it deserves."

As Paul exited, Tom entered.

"The door, Tom, the door. Do you see the door? It's meant to keep people from bursting in. Now, please close the door on your way out and don't barge in."

Sheepishly Tom backed out and closed the door. Confused, he remained there for a moment and then knocked.

"Not now. I'm busy."

Tom knocked harder.

"For God's sakes, come in. What's so important?"

"Ira, there are two men here to see you."

"We go to press in an hour. Ask them to come back later or leave a message."

"I think you need to see them."

"Why? Do they own our newspaper?"

"They're with the FBI."

"The FBI?"

"The FBI!"

"Did they say what they want?"

"No. Just that they want to see you."

"They want to see me personally, or me as Editor?"

"I have no idea."

"OK, send them in."

As Tom withdrew, Ira donned his jacket and straightened out his desk. Moments later Tom returned, followed closely by William Taylor and Jeffrey Dotson, a younger clone of Taylor. Ira immediately noticed the younger man trying to emulate the more senior agent in both dress and demeanor, yet seeming to retain a look of perpetual confusion on his face.

"Ira, these gentlemen are from the FBI. Gentlemen, this is Ira Lewis, Managing Editor of the *Courier*."

"Gentlemen!"

Ira knew the older man, Taylor, would be the spokesman. The other man was likely there for show or training or whatever.

"Mr. Lewis, thank you for seeing us. I'm William Taylor and this is Jeffrey Dotson. We're from the Washington, D.C. Office of the Federal Bureau of Investigation."

"Please, sit down. Can I get you some coffee?"

Jeffrey Dotson started to accept but when Taylor declined, he quickly decided to follow suit.

"And why have senior FBI agents traveled from Washington D.C. to visit a Negro, non-subversive, newspaper in industrialized Pennsylvania?"

"The *Courier* is one of the largest Black newspapers in the country. It exerts enormous influence."

"We try to impart the news to our readers, yes, but whether we exert enormous influence is questionable. Either way, I'm glad the FBI thinks so. But, continue, please."

"The tone of some of the recent articles your paper has printed have raised some concerns and Mr. Hoover thought an informal conversation was the best way to handle it."

"Tone? I'm sorry, Mr. Taylor. What do you mean by tone?"

"Your articles that reference The Double V. They strike a tone that seems to becoming a serious distraction to the war effort."

"Well, our paper has no desire to cause concern to the Bureau or any other Federal Department."

"Good! Good! Thank you. Senator Guffey told us you'd be most cooperative. And, I'm sure that Mr. Hoover will appreciate it as well."

"But perhaps you can clarify who or what we're distracting, so I fully understand."

"The country must have a unified message. Build more tanks and planes. Get more men into uniform. Here it is,

1942, just a few months short of one year since Pearl Harbor and we still haven't maximized production. It's going to take every one of our nearly 150 million Americans focusing on winning this war."

"Well, no one could disagree with that. Let me ask Miss Chandler to join us. She should be in on this conversation."

Ira stood, went to the door and motioned Erma to come in. She responded with a nod of her head, 'No, I don't want to join you.' Ira's frown could be seen by the entire office. Paul had told her that Ira's visitors were from the FBI and she had no desire to join the conversation. This next time Ira shouted and Erma moved reluctantly toward his office.

"Gentlemen, this is Miss Erma Chandler. Erma, these gentlemen are from the FBI. It's Miss Chandler who first uncovered the letter that launched our Double V campaign. She understood the importance of its meaning."

"How do you do, Miss Chandler," Taylor said. "I've seen your byline on a number of the articles and I understand you've met with the young man who wrote it."

"I did, and you can tell from his letter that he loves this country. He's very patriotic and just wants to serve."

"I like your writing Miss Chandler."

"Thank you, Mister..."

"Dotson, Jefferson Dotson."

"Thank you, Mr. Dotson."

"Erma, Mr. Taylor thinks our Double V campaign is detracting from the country's focus on the war. What do you think?"

"I'm sorry, Mr. Lewis, Miss Chandler," Taylor interrupted. "We're not here to debate the issue. The government, your government, wants you to cease your Double V campaign and focus on the war. It's spread to dozens of other papers and celebrities. It's a diversion and the country doesn't need it."

"On the contrary," Erma interrupted. "It's all about the war. Getting Negroes into the war and into the factories."

Moments ago, things had been going well. Now this woman comes in and the agents found themselves in the middle of a debate. Taylor's irritation and voice both rose. "It's race, and you know it. Pitting blacks against whites."

Now it was Ira's turn to voice his feelings. "We already pit blacks against whites. Government housing projects, employment...they all favor whites over blacks."

"I don't set government policy, Miss Chandler, Mr. Lewis."

"Neither does the *Courier* but if we don't raise our voice to injustice, it will continue," Erma pleaded.

"Erma's right, gentlemen. All we're asking is that the country ignore the color of a man's skin and focus on the war. Negroes want to fight."

"We want to prove we're equal Americans in this struggle."

"Let me say it again," Taylor said, moving to the edge of his seat. "The Federal Government insists on a unified message to the public. Your campaign is distracting from that effort. Where issues of racism arise, war production declines. That's a plain, unvarnished fact."

"No one wants that, but Negroes are sitting on the sideline. Get them into the factories and production will climb."

"Rhetoric aside, if you can't get on board, Mr. Hoover has other measures he's prepared to take."

"Mr. Taylor, a large segment of the population supports the Double V."

"It needs to stop."

"We can't do that."

"Other Negro-owned newspapers have agreed to cut back on the Double V references and focus on the war effort," Jeffrey Dotson said in a more conciliatory voice.

"They didn't launch the Double V, Mr. Dotson, we did!" Erma said as the conversation had now become a four-sided free-for-all.

"Well, now the government is asking you to un-launch it" Bill Taylor insisted.

"You are aiding and abetting those who do not want America to win this war by distracting the people with issues about equality," Dotson pleaded.

Both Ira and William Taylor were standing now. Each knew the other was right but neither was willing or able to alter their position, whether war and patriotism would trump morality?

"Mr. Taylor!", Ira insisted. "All colored people want is a recognition of the rights we were given by the 13th, 14th, and 15th Amendments of the Constitution."

"Mr. Lewis!"

"Mr. Taylor!"

"I am here representing Mr. Hoover, the Federal Bureau of Investigation, the Justice Department and the President of the United States."

"I understand," Ira sighed, trying to calm the tone of the overheated conversation. "And we try to represent Freedom of Speech..."

"...and Freedom of the Press, particularly for minorities," Erma added.

Taylor took a breath. He tried to calm himself or he and Dotson would be leaving this office without an agreement. Mr. Hoover would not be happy. He turned back to try a softer approach.

"We appreciate the delicacy of our request. We value both freedom of speech and freedom of the press. But we are trying to ensure every one's freedom by winning the war."

"Mr. Taylor, get us into this war," Erma pleaded. "Give colored people an opportunity to be treated as equals."

"I'm sure you don't think that Mr. Hoover or anyone in the FBI condones racism in any form."

"I certainly hope not."

"You have to find another forum. Your Double V campaign is divisive. We're just messengers. Stop the program."

"Thank you for coming," Ira said as he stood, needing to end the meeting. "Our regards to Mr. Hoover."

Erma found herself shaking as the FBI men departed. These men represented the government and they'd left here very unhappy. It was a frightening experience.

"Ira, I'm too young for jail and too old for Juvenile Hall."

"You aren't going to jail."

"Are you sure?"

"Not really!"

"Can we keep doing what we've been doing?"

"Until they shut us down."

Erma folded herself into Ira's arms and remained. She could hear Ira's heartbeat and she understood they had taken a very difficult position. Their future and the future of the *Courier* had become very uncertain.

Chapter Twenty

Annie had come over early and fixed a scrumptious dinner. She'd even baked an Apple Brown Betty for dessert. Clyde had retired early, and now she and Jimmy were sitting on the couch listening to the radio. Edward R. Murrow was broadcasting from London and you could hear bombs exploding in the background. Upset, Annie got up and played with the dial until she found soft sounds from New York's Roseland theatre.

"I'd rather listen to music. All the news is too depressing. I want things to be the way they were last year."

"Well, that's not going to happen anytime soon," Jimmy said, turning down the lights and taking Annie's hand, pulling her down beside him.

"What a difference a few months has made. This time last year we were talking about you returning to college, and then us maybe get married," she looked directly at this man she loved so much. "You're not planning on returning to college in the fall, are you?"

"No. No matter how I add things up, our plans for college and marriage have all been upended by the war. With guys fightin' and dyin' in the far corners of the world, everything's changed. It just doesn't feel right being a passive observer, sitting on the sidelines."

"I've never known you to be passive about anything important."

"I'm not passive about you," he smiled, kissing her lightly on the lips.

"I guess that makes me important," she said, nestling closer, their cheeks touching.

"You are definitely on my most important list," he smiled, kissing her sweetly.

"I do like being important."

Jimmy stood and walked into the kitchen for two Cokes. He returned, handing one to Annie.

"Did I tell you the bosses at Cessna are nervous about my letter having an impact on them getting new contracts for airplanes?"

"Why? What happened?"

"It seems the President of Cessna got a phone call from the FBI wanting to know more about the person who wrote the letter that got printed in the *Pittsburgh Courier*."

"And the *Courier* led them back to you!"

"Had to be! Anyway, Charlie says the only reason I wasn't fired is something about Cessna not wanting to have a race problem. With new Army contracts pending they don't want any negative publicity."

"So, you weren't fired? What are they going to do?"

"Probably nothing, but Charlie was pretty clear that they don't want any more letters. I ended up having to speak to his supervisor."

"Was he nice?"

"Not particularly. He made it clear I was causing trouble and the bosses weren't happy with me."

"What did you say?"

"I didn't say much but I did ask him if he could help me enlist. I reminded him it was the easiest way to get rid of me."

"Pretty clever...and?"

"He's a 60-year-old, brain-dead white guy they pulled from retirement. He kind'a just looked at me, confused. I don't think he could understand why I'd prefer the Army to working at Cessna. Annie, I need to get into the war. Really into the war...not just another 'colored boy' cleaning latrines or saying 'Yes sir,' 'No, sir.' to a white officer."

"I never knew you felt so strongly about race and prejudice and all those things."

"Until the war came I didn't. But then I saw those newsreels of Jap planes killing Americans. White boys lining up, volunteering. Not a single person who looked like me was up on that screen. Damn it, Annie. It made me angry. The entire white part of this country is cranking up for war, and we're invisible. I can feel it at the factory and in the attitude of people like Charlie."

"Charlie just likes to bluster. Makes him feel like a big man."

"Maybe, but there are other 'crackers' he hangs with who think the same way. Superior! Entitled! And, sometimes they can be dangerous... like 'Walk on the other side of the street when a white's coming'. 'Don't you dare look at a white woman'."

Meanwhile, outside on the front lawn in the dark, three men had gathered. They'd been wearing white hoods but had removed them. It made it too difficult to argue and take care of this 'uppity nigger.'

"We burning a cross in the lawn or not," one of them asked impatiently.

151

"Keep your voice down, damn it! We'll burn the cross later, closer to morning, after they're all asleep. Meanwhile I want to make sure they get the message." He was clearly the one in charge and the other two deferred to him."

"Pete, won't the fire give him the message?"

"No names. How many times have I told you, no names?

"Sorry, Pete. I keep forgetting."

"Well, try remembering."

Pete worked at the Cessna factory and after talking to Charlie, it was pretty clear just talking to this piss-ant kid wouldn't be enough.

"Can you get it through that window?" Pete asked.

"You've seen me throw a baseball and that window is a hell of a lot closer."

"OK, the note's attached. Let it go!"

The rock sailed the 20' into the bedroom window. The men laughed, patted one another on the back and scattered to the old pick-up truck they'd parked around the corner.

In the living room Jimmy and Annie heard the breaking of glass. Jimmy rushed through the front door to confront whoever had done it but the men were already gone. He could hear the sound of a truck speeding away. Jimmy went back inside to make sure everyone was alright.

Clyde emerged from his bedroom, wearing his old tattered robe and slippers and holding a rock.

"Woke me from my sleep, bastards."

"Dad, are you O.K.?"

"I'm O.K. You see who did it?"

"No, they must have just thrown the rock and taken off. No sign of them."

"Crackers! Looks like they attached a note. Here, you read it, I don't have my reading glasses."

"This rock is a warning. Writin' letters tryin' to change the natural order of things can be dangerous."

"I knew that letter of yours could cause problems," Clyde said, shaking his head.

"You said that, but I thought you were exaggerating. We probably need to be cautious. I wouldn't want anything bad to happen to either of you."

"Do you think they might come back?" Annie asked.

"I don't know, Annie. I don't have any experience with things like this."

"All over a letter. Who could guess? I guess you stirred up more than colored folks. Seems you've also angered white folks as well."

"Most white folks like things just like they are...them on top and us ruttin' 'round in the dirt," Clyde added. "They'd like things to stay the way they've always been."

"So, what do we do?"

"I don't think we do anything," Jimmy said. "The letter is out there and The Double V is moving on its own momentum."

"Well, I'm goin' to clean up that glass and try to get back to sleep. Jimmy, promise me you ain't writin' any more letters tonight."

"I promise," Jimmy said, happy no one was hurt.

Clyde turned as he left the room, "Your mother would have been proud of what you wrote, Jimmy. You did good."

Chapter Twenty-One

William Taylor was working through a stack of files when Jeffrey Dotson entered, his brow furrowed and damp.

"Bill, there's been a double lynching. A really bad one this time."

"Jeff, trust me, there's never been a good lynching."

"I guess. This one is scary bad. A small town in Mississippi... Shubuta! Two thirteen-year-old colored boys. They'd been seen talking to a 13-year-old white girl. Girl's father said the boys molested her, and demanded the local Sheriff arrest the two boys and charge them with rape. He wouldn't even allow the Sheriff to talk to the young girl to get her side of the story."

"Damn small-town cops. I wouldn't hire a one of them to clean a shit house, much less run a police department. Did the boys confess?"

"No. The Sheriff admitted he talked to the boys for more than six hours. Their story never changed. They said they were just talkin' to the girl, nothing more. I mean, that's what kids do. The girl was never touched. "

"I hate to see what the *Courier* is going to do with this story. It's right up their alley. This could ignite a lot of racial violence. We can probably get the white newspapers to not report the story but the Black press will definitely run with it."

"I'm afraid there's more."

"My God! What else?"

"The next evening the girl's father and a group of other whites forced the Sheriff to turn the boys over to them. They beat and mutilated the two boys something awful. Then they took their bodies to the Shubuta railroad bridge and lynched them."

"Jesus! What kind of hate-filled insanity exists in people like that?"

"Has to be a hatred that they're taught at a very early age. God help us all."

Frank had brought the same story to Ira's attention and the reaction was one of dismay and the abject failure of the system to protect children eighty years after slavery had been abolished.

"Frank, write it up, front page. We need to tell the world that these were just innocent young boys."

"What about the quote from the Sheriff?"

"Absolutely! And a picture of the son-of-a-bitch with the caption…'Sanctioned Murder'."

"I understand the big white newspapers have been told to lay off the story for fear of rioting."

"Sure! Sweep it under the rug. Well, we're not one of those papers. Black folks need to share our outrage and shame on the white press for agreeing to ignore the story."

Erma entered and seeing how depressed Ira was, she moved behind him to rub his shoulders and, hopefully, ease the obvious tension she could see in his face.

"Whatever it is, it can't be that bad."

"Actually, it can. Small town in Mississippi! Two innocent boys got mutilated and then lynched, bodies hung from an old railroad bridge."

"Are we running the story?"

"Big and bold! It won't make Mr. Hoover and his friends at the FBI very happy but I really don't give a shit. This was just too horrific."

"Is the FBI ever happy?"

"Probably not. Those wing tip shoes they wear probably pinch their toes. Oh, rub more! That's it, the left side."

Ira stood, shook himself, and tried to regain his equilibrium.

"Erma, I need to break our date this weekend."

"Want to tell me why?"

"Frank scored tickets to see Joe Louis fight at Madison Square Garden."

"You're going all the way to New York to see a prize fight?"

"Please don't give me attitude? It's a hell'uva lot closer than Wichita."

"It's a boxing match."

"I used to be the Sports Editor of this paper and you obviously don't understand. This is Joe Louis, the Brown Bomber, the heavyweight champion of the world. When he fought Buddy Baer last month, he sent the guy to the hospital. He is THE colored champion and now he's Private Joe Louis with fists that come out of nowhere."

"Well, you boys have fun watching two oversize men pummel one another."

"We will."

Erma started to leave, upset, when Ira smiled.

"Don't get into trouble while I'm gone."

"Said by a man who's going to play in New York City for a weekend."

Erma found herself with a free weekend. She could visit her family, tour the city, or just relax and go to a movie. She climbed the stairs and entered the lobby. Bessie was busy, dusting pictures.

"Hi, Bessie," she said.

"Hi, baby, how you doin'? Got big plans this weekend?"

"Not really. I haven't seen my family in a while. I was thinking of renting a car now that I have a driver's license and visiting them. Say, why don't you come with me? It would do us both good."

"I'm not sure I can leave this place."

Erma was warming to the idea. Her father and Bessie would be quite a pair. "This old building won't go anywhere, I promise. We'll leave tomorrow morning and come back Sunday afternoon."

Erma rented a 1938 Plymouth and they headed south for Fayette. The car rental man had given her maps and directions. Bessie was all 'gussied up.' She'd fixed sandwiches for

158

them both and the car had a good radio. Bessie knew all the songs and the two women sang their way across Pennsylvania.

Saturday evening and most of Sunday Erma watched her father, a Preacher, laugh with a woman who spent her life singing in brothels and liquor-filled clubs. It was magic. She and her brothers had gone to sleep hours before the two elders ran out of energy, regaling stories of surviving the depression.

Monday morning Erma was back at her desk writing a piece about being black during the depression, trying to remember some of the stories her father and Bessie had shared. She looked up and there was Ira and Frank, walking in, clearly frazzled.

"Well, well, the Hardy boys have returned from their New York adventure. Will we see an article soon? Maybe even a picture spread in National Geographic?"

"Absolutely. I wrote it on the train. Great fight, but I suppose you need to be a guy to appreciate the manly art of fisticuffs."

"Right, hairy legs, lots of sweating and swearing. Gee, you men have all the luck."

"Erma sounds jealous, doesn't she?" Frank Bolden smiled.

"She probably needs a good bake sale to report on. Anyway, we have work to do. Erma, can I see you?"

She followed Ira into his office.

"Erma, I need a break. I never realized the pressure Bob Vann was under every day. And since we launched the Double V campaign, every decision seems huge. You do remember I told you I used to be THE sports writer for the *Courier*, don't you? Well, I still have some pretty good contacts and I have a chance to interview a couple of promising colored baseball players in Chicago. As long as I'm going that far, how about I boogie down to Wichita and meet our Jimmy Thompson?"

"Sure. Want me to "boogie" with you?"

"Why not? We both need to get away from here."

"Who are you going to be interviewing?"

"You probably never heard of them. Two promising kids, Nate Moreland and Jack Robinson."

"Jack Robinson? As in Jackie Robinson?"

"He's the one. The Chicago White sox are going to let the two of them play a couple of preseason games with the team. They want to see how the fans react to seeing black and white players on the field together."

"I'd love to see baseball integrated but with all the anger in the country, it could be a big problem...riots, boycotts. The thought of white fans having one too many beers when a pitch is too close to a white hitter, or someone sliding into second with his spikes up. No, I do love baseball but not with the racism that still exists. How do you get people to accept blacks and whites on the same team when we're still writing stories about two thirteen-year-old colored boys getting lynched?"

"Either way, the Sox and Jackie will make a good story, and, who knows, we might even have time to ka-noodle."

Chapter Twenty-Two

Three days in Chicago were just the refreshment Ira and Erma needed. The interviews went well and they got to see the White Sox play the Yankees from seats in the Press Box. They even had time to ka-noodle before taking the train to Wichita.

They exited the cab, approached the front door and rang the bell.

"Erma, welcome back."

"Nice to see you again, Jimmy. This is my boss and the Publisher of the *Courier*, Ira Lewis."

"Mr. Lewis. Welcome to Wichita. Is this your first visit?"

"It is. And it's nice to finally meet you. I've done a lot of wondering about what sort of young man could write such an impressive letter. The way Erma described you was most complimentary."

"Come in, Mr. Lewis. I'd like you to meet my fiance', Annie Culver."

"Nice to meet you, Mr. Lewis. Hi Erma. Can I get either of you some refreshments?"

"I think we're fine. Jimmy, we brought you a present from Chicago."

"A present?"

"We interviewed a couple of promising young Negro league baseball players and they signed this baseball "to the Double V" along with the entire Chicago White Sox team."

"That's real nice. Look, Annie. One of them was Jackie Robinson. You know who he is?"

"He was a football star at UCLA."

"And baseball."

"And baseball. He batted .320 last year for Honolulu in the Negro league after he graduated."

"How did you know that?" Jimmy asking, grinning.

"My Dad always read the sports page to me growing up."

"You never fail to amaze me. My Dad and I used to drive up to see the Kansas City Monarchs every chance we got. They've always been one of the top teams in the Negro League. Those were wonderful weekends."

"Jackie got drafted by the Monarchs but before he could play, he got drafted by the Army and that took precedence. He reports in six weeks for Basic Training. He also told me that he'd applied to be an Officer because he had his Bachelor's degree but the Army is blocking all Negro applications to become officers."

"The good news is that the entire Negro League has adopted the Double V. They'll be wearing the logo on their uniforms and promoting it in every baseball program."

Jimmy smiled, bouncing the ball up and down from hand to hand, uncomfortably distracted.

"What's the matter, Jimmy? Erma and I thought you'd be excited about all the excitement and support your letter has generated. We're getting reactions from Hollywood to New York," Ira said. "They all agree with you, Jimmy. Isn't that something?"

"It is, Mr. Lewis. It's all very thrilling but look at it from my side. Jackie Robinson's biggest problem is becoming an officer. At least he got drafted and he's in the Army. They won't even let me enlist. It isn't fair."

"Lots of things in life aren't fair. You know that. Your letter said it. There are two Americas. It's going to happen! It really is and your letter is helping speed up the process. California just started drafting Negroes...a sort of experiment. It's coming. They need to set up separate training bases and barracks. And who trains you...whites or coloreds? At this time, it has to be whites. There aren't enough Negroes in uniforms to fill a room."

"I'm a terrible hostess," Annie said, standing. "Let me go get us some refreshments."

"That's a wonderful idea. I can help," Erma added, following Annie into the kitchen.

Annie busied herself finding platters and arranging food from the refrigerator as Erma watched. Suddenly Annie dropped a glass platter. She stood, frozen, watching it shatter on the floor. Then, suddenly, she burst into tears.

"Annie, it's only a platter. Here, let me help clean it up."

163

"It isn't the platter, Erma. I'm finding it hard to keep it together. I'm just so conflicted. Jimmy is intent on getting into the war and I don't want him to leave me. He could get killed and I'd never see him again."

"Annie, men across the globe are being pulled into this conflict whether they want to or not. Meanwhile, women everywhere are forced to share the same fear of loss. Mothers, sisters, wives and girlfriends. All of us. We're all part of a very sad sisterhood."

"I suppose so."

"That's what wars have always done. Men leave and some don't return."

"Then what are we supposed to do?"

"We give them a reason to come home. Love, children, a safe haven. We try and lift their spirits. I can't imagine Jimmy not wanting to come home to you."

"It's so difficult."

"No one said it's easy. But it is necessary. Now, what do we have to eat?"

Chapter Twenty-Three

Calm and decorum had been tossed out the window. J. Edgar Hoover, with a carefully calculated reputation for always giving serious consideration to the issues, had lost it. He was shouting at a cowering William Taylor and Jefferson Dotson, threatening firing, transfers to Anchorage or simple decapitation.

"All I asked you to do was convince a Negro newspaper editor to soften a promotional program called the Double V. A junior agent should have been able to get it done and you two dunderheads have succeeded in The Double V becoming a national symbol. Nice job!"

"Mr. Hoover..."

"Taylor, don't interrupt when I'm venting."

"Yes, sir."

"And don't call me 'sir'."

Hoover paced his office, poured some water from a carafe and swallowed it down with two pills from an unmarked bottle that rested nearby.

"Now the son of a bitch has convinced the entire Negro baseball league to wear a Double V patch...and promote it in their program. We're lucky he didn't convince the White Sox to integrate baseball while he was in Chicago."

"I'm sure he tried," Dotson added, wanting to feel part of the conversation.

"Every edition he prints demands Proportional Representation. The Southern Senators won't tolerate it and if they block it, Roosevelt has no chance of getting it approved. The President asked me to perform a simple task, move a slogan out of the limelight. Instead, senior agents of the FBI have allowed it to be lit in neon lights."

"We tried, Mr. Hoover. The man won't move," Taylor begged.

"Damn it, it's affecting production at major factories. Generals and Admirals are complaining they need more of everything and they need it now. No more conversations. I want that damn paper silenced."

"We can sue him."

"Takes too long. You get a hold of Byron Price. He runs the Office of Censorship. He has the authority to close the *Courier*. Tell him we need it done."

"Yes, sir."

Byron Price, hair greying at the temples, heavy tortoise-rimmed glasses and wearing an expensive Brooks Bros. suit, arrived at the *Pittsburgh Courier* offices along with William Taylor. Price had been plucked from his position as head of the Associated Press wire services to head the Office of Censorship. Not a job he wanted, but the request had come directly from the Oval office.

In a nutshell his job was to make certain movies, radio, and newspapers, the primary sources of communication, told the 'American First,' 'Patriotism is Everything' story. Movies were to show American bravery, as well as the courage of our allies, Great Britain, China and Russia. They were also encouraged to portray the depravity of the Axis powers, bombing children, and ignoring conventions regarding the treatment of prisoners of war. Movies like Mission to Moscow, lauding Stalin and Russia were already in Production. A war movie focusing on Japanese atrocities, The Purple Heart, had already been green-lighted.

On the home front Communist and Socialists were not going to be allowed to foment discontent. Included in that category was anything that would stoke racial discord. Byron Price had come to Pittsburgh from Washington, D.C. to personally make sure that Ira Lewis understood the consequences of his Double V and Proportional Representation campaign.

"Byron Price? My God, what dragged you away from Washington?" Frank Bolden asked, surprised to see his old friend walk through the door.

"Hello, Frank. Oh, they let me out of the D.C zoo occasionally."

"You must have done something awful."

"I wouldn't be surprised. Whatever I do is wrong to half the country."

"You know, Byron, I submitted an application to be a War Correspondent."

"Yes, I know. But aren't you a little old to slog around in the mud with 19-year-old kids?"

"Nah! I'm in my prime. How about it? I'm serious. I don't want to see this war in newsreels. Please, have your people take it seriously."

"Let me see what I can do."

"Thanks. Now, why are you here?"

"How many guesses do you need" Price asked sarcastically.

"Actually, we're all surprised you haven't been here sooner," Frank nodded somberly.

"This is Bill Taylor, with the FBI. I think he's been here before, haven't you Bill?"

"I have," he said, unsmiling. We're here to see Ira Lewis... again."

"Of course, you are."

"The FBI thinks the *Courier* has carried this Double V campaign too far. They've asked me to come up here to explain to Ira what can happen to the *Courier* if he remains intransigent."

"Ira? Intransigent? Say it isn't so."

"Mr. Lewis will see you now," Erma announced as she approached the small group.

"Mind if I join you?" Frank asked. "Whatever gets decided affects all of us. We've all been part of the Double V and I have to tell you, Byron, I've become a believer in the need to bring the Negro population into the war."

"Sure, join us, if Ira doesn't mind. We're all good friends."

"Byron Price!" Ira said, standing as the small group paraded into his office. "Oh, my, they've sent the big guns. Hello, Mr. Taylor. If you've come to tar and feather me, we might as well begin."

"How have you been, Ira?" Price said, speaking in his usual casual style. He was not a shouter. "It's been at least two years...the Associated Press conference, May 1940? "

"I think you're right. The world has changed a lot since then, hasn't it? Sit, all of you. It looks as if you've done well, Byron."

"If you call trading a plush, high paying, job for a dollar-a-year government gig doing well, it has. I was sorry to hear about Robert Vann's passing. He was a terrific newspaper man. A real force."

"Yes, it was a huge loss."

"Ira, I'm not happy to be here."

"I know. I'm sorry it has all come to this."

"What do we need to do to get us all on the same page? I mean, we all have the same objective. Winning the war. Getting our country back to normal."

"That's true but, I'm afraid we deviate on what winning the war means. And as Jimmy Thompson's letter implies, we're actually fighting two wars. Did you read his letter, Byron?"

"I did, and I don't deny it's power. Racism is one of our country's failures but we've allowed our enemies to rearm and threaten our democracy. We're already fighting on two fronts, the Pacific and Europe. We don't have the ability to fight on a third front, domestic racism, at the same time."

"The Double V. A V for victory in the war, V for victory in racial equality at home" Catchy! People remember it. It sounds...," Ira searched for the right word. "Fair! We all like 'fair,' don't we, Byron? We don't see it as a third front. We see it as a way to shorten the war."

"Coloreds want to fight, prove their patriotism," Erma added.

"Mr. Lewis, if you read your own newspaper, coloreds are being hired in record numbers to work in defense factories."

"Yes, Negro unemployment is down. And it looks as if more Negroes will be accepted for military duty. BUT there are still lynchings in the south, rioting at housing developments in the north and fights wherever colored soldiers are stationed. We are seeking equality at home, Mr. Taylor. Is that too much to ask?"

"Ira...," Price tried to interject.

Ignoring the interruption, Ira continued, his temperature and rhetoric rising.

"You'd prefer that millions of Negroes continue to be patient."

"Yes! At least until the war is over."

"And what do our people get for this display of patience?" Frank asked.

"Get? We all get a military victory," Taylor said. "Isn't that the most important thing?"

"Not if it returns an entire segment of the population to poll taxes, prejudice, and Jim Crow laws."

Byron Price stood and the room went quiet. They were all friends, members of the same profession, the same fraternity, reporters of the human condition.

"You want to change society. I'm with you but that's way beyond us. What we do know is that everywhere race issues explode, factory production declines. Can you imagine what could follow? Armies short of weapons, outnumbered in the skies, more battle losses, more Gold Star mothers. We're at war, for God's sakes, and our very way of life is at stake."

"Byron, we understand that, we do, and each and every Negro in this nation shares your concern but our society needs changing. You know that. You want us to continue to ignore insults, violence, unfair treatment. You want to exclude ten percent of your citizens from helping achieve our mutual goal, ending the war."

"If that's what it takes to maximize the war effort, that may be necessary and I can live with it," Bill Taylor said with a belligerency that felt like fingers scratching a blackboard.

"Are you a racist, Mr. Taylor?" Erma asked.

"I don't think so."

"Many Negro agents in the FBI?"

"I'm not sure."

170

"Any colored friends?" Erma persisted.

"My personal life isn't relevant."

"Actually, Erma's questions are relevant," Ira stepped in. "Your position...Mr. Hoover's position, and probably most white people, deal with racism and prejudice as unfortunate, and since you all would never consciously cross a street to avoid a Negro, it's all those "other" people."

"Ira, please," Price pleaded. "Philosophy aside, we're dealing with a specific issue today."

"I'm sorry, Bryan. It's more than that. Attitudes have to change. White America can't continue to pretend we don't exist. Let Negroes fight alongside Whites, play on the same sports team, live next door. Let their children play together."

"Ira, Erma. I would do it in a moment if I could snap my fingers and make it happen. I share your frustrations. I do. But I can't. Your campaign has to end or it will be necessary to use the government's authority under the War Powers Act to force the *Courier* to stop using the war to influence social change. We could just plain shut you down."

"Understood! But if you do, the government will be following the same path they did in Nazi Germany. Killing a free press. Go ahead! You will probably win but we will raise a hell of a lot of noise." Ira's eyes had teared, his voice breaking. His thoughts strayed momentarily to a picture of those two young boys hanging from the Shubata bridge.

"The American Negro has been under the yolk of a 'separate but equal' policy that has kept us separate but never equal," Ira continued. "That's a war also. And if our country's war ends without some changes the young Negro men in this country will have shed their blood in vain."

171

"The last thing we need right now is hot headed whites and coloreds focusing on one another instead of united to fight Germany and the Japs," Taylor added.

"Then help us," Ira pleaded.

"Ira, the government will shut you down. No one wants that. We're asking for a patriotic focus. Get your head around it. Our country is threatened and that trumps racial divides."

"I understand. The *Courier* will end its Double V campaign once Negroes are given a chance to fully participate in defending our great country. "

Everyone in the room was exhausted. Each side, argued with passion, had failed to sway the other. Byron Price stood and Bill Taylor followed.

"Ira, it's been good seeing you. You and your staff are carrying a noble banner into battle. We're not on the same side but I wish you luck."

Chapter Twenty-Four

The news staff of the *Courier* continued to work. No one discussed Byron Price's visit for fear that any mention would jinx them and speed up a government closure. Weeks passed. Erma was at her typewriter when Cory entered, wearing a Navy dress uniform. Erma screamed when she saw him.

"Cory! Cory Phelps! Oh, my God. Look at you."

"Ensign Cory Phelps, United States Navy, if you please?"

"What are you doing here?"

"I came to take you and Wendall to lunch? I just finished training and I ship out in a few days. I didn't want to leave without connecting."

"You know, you're very handsome in that uniform."

"Of course, I am."

"And modest."

"Lunch?"

"I'd be delighted but I'm not sure where Wendall is?"

"Then I'll have you all to myself."

They grabbed a cab for a short ride to the restaurant, a small French bistro filled with business people, tired shoppers, and men in an array of military uniforms.

"Wine?" Cory asked.

"No. This is the middle of the day and I'm a working girl."

"Well, you look lovely, older, but still buoyant with self-confidence. Playing any baseball?"

"No, but I am a full-fledged reporter."

"I know. I've been reading some of your articles. That young man from Wichita certainly lit a fire, didn't he?"

"Jimmy Thompson! He certainly did, and now the government wants us to stop pushing the Double V or else."

"Or else?"

"Seems they can shut us down under some wartime censorship act they'd passed."

"That's pretty drastic."

"Have you heard of Proportional Representation?"

"I have. That's one of the reasons I wanted to see you."

"Not just my ebullient personality?"

"Well, of course that, too," he smiled. "Look, the Navy has been circulating a secret memo and a friend showed it to me. They're planning to open enlistments to men of all races effective in August."

"All races? No way."

"Way! They're being dragged screaming into the 20th century. They need men."

"My God, Cory. This is big news. Any idea when they're going to announce it?"

"No, I'm a lowly ensign but it's definitely soon."

Back at the *Courier* Tom and Wendall were chatting.

"Hey, Wendall, get this. Just came off the news wire. The Army is rounding up all the Japs on the West Coast and putting them into Internment Camps?"

"No shit?" Wendall said, surprised. "That's pretty radical. Why?"

"In case they're Jap spies. I don't really know."

174

"Can the government do that...just pick up groups of citizens?"

"I don't know...sounds scary."

"Sounds like Nazi Germany," Wendall moaned.

"Does that mean that if we get into a war with an African country, we'll get jailed 'cause 'all niggers look alike to white folk'?"

Wendall laughed at the idea, "Nah! Who would clean all the sewers, pick up the garbage, and take care of the kids?"

The two reporters were still laughing as Erma rushed in, pulling Cory along. She stormed into Ira's office as Cory and Wendall tried to greet one another. Wendall and Tom followed her into Ira's office.

"Why do I even have a door if people are going to barge in without knocking?"

"Ira, you remember Cory, don't you?"

"No. And please don't just burst into my office. I'd really appreciate a little respect and protocol."

"A little...right. Cory was the pitcher on our baseball team."

"Oh, right! Sorry, Cory. I didn't recognize you in the uniform."

"Cory heard some interesting scuttlebutt."

"Scuttlebutt we can print?"

"Not my decision."

"Tell him!"

"The Navy is throwing enlistments open to everyone, regardless of race."

"Really! Wow," Wendall said, his eyes dancing. "Maybe I can get me one of those jazzy uniforms."

"I'm not sure the Navy will be that desperate," Cory laughed. "Anyway, it's happening sometime very soon."

"Let's gamble and leak it," Ira said. "You know, 'reliable sources tell us.'"

"I'm on it."

"Wait a minute! I want something for the story," Cory said.

Erma hesitated, confused. "I don't understand."

"Dinner and dancing at the Savoy this evening, you and me."

Erma took a moment to process and breathed a sigh of relief.

"You've got it."

Ira didn't like that this white naval officer had invited his girlfriend to dinner. He was even more upset that she accepted. He fumed in silence.

Cory and Erma arrived at a fashionable 9 o'clock, just as the orchestra took the stage. He was still in his dress blues. Erma's wardrobe had matured and her off the shoulder emerald dress was striking. When the dishes from the main course were removed, Cory stood and reached for Erma's hand, leading her onto the dance floor. Within seconds a large well-dressed colored man approached them.

"Excuse me! I'm cutting in."

Erma put her hands on her hips, irate. "Again? Buzz off! This is my brother and he's leaving for combat next week. He's also a black belt in Judo so he'd probably kick your ass."

"Excuse me, I didn't know," the man said, retreating.

"That's why I love you. You have such a soft, feminine demeanor."

When the music ended, Cory led Erma outside to the balcony and kissed her.

"Cory!"

"Don't say anything. We'll talk when the war's over."

Chapter Twenty-Five

Annie was sitting in the living room reading a magazine. The most popular songs from around the country were on her favorite radio program, The Lucky Strike Hit Parade. It played softly in the background.

Jimmy entered quietly, hoping Annie wouldn't see him. His heart was palpitating, his hands were damp. He wanted it to be a good surprise but he was afraid it would be an unhappy shock.

"Annie, close your eyes. Turn around slowly."

Annie turned slowly.

"Don't open them yet."

Jimmy positioned himself, straightened his uniform and donned his cap.

"O.K. You can open your eyes."

Annie followed Jimmy's instructions and opened her eyes. She jumped up in shock and caught her breath. Jimmy, her Jimmy, was standing there in front of her in an Army khaki uniform.

"Jimmy! Jimmy! What have you done?"

Jimmy laughed as if he were an eight-year-old with a new Lionel train set.

"When? How? Why didn't you tell me?"

"Sit down and I will. It all happened so fast and until it actually happened, I didn't want to jinx it by saying anything."

"OK! Tell me! I'm waiting."

"It may have been Ira Lewis but it could have been Jackie Robinson, I'm not sure who but I got a call from Ira about a week ago asking if I could get to Kansas City. It seems one of the owners of the Kansas City Monarchs baseball team was also on the local enlistment board. Ira said the man agreed to help me if I could get there."

"If he's on the Enlistment Board, he's probably white!"

"Probably. I don't know for sure. Anyway, I convinced my father to take a day off and drive up with me. I didn't meet the man but I did go the enlistment board and apply. They accepted me. They never mentioned that I was colored, they didn't seem to care. They just looked at me, gave me a simple physical and said I was 1-A. Just like that I was in the Army. Me, James Thompson, was now Private James Thompson, United States Army."

Annie turned silent, fighting back tears, turning away from Jimmy so he wouldn't notice.

"Annie, please be happy for me. You know I needed to do this."

"I do. But it was never now. It was just some vague thing that was going to happen. Suddenly, it's here and I'm just now realizing you're going to go away, probably to somewhere with a name I can't pronounce. And our plans..."

Jimmy pulled Annie, gently, to her feet, wiped away a tear and held her as she sobbed.

"Our plans haven't changed," he said softly. "They're just on hold. We'll be fine."

"'Fine' being alone isn't the same as 'fine' being together."

"You still want to get married, don't you? Even though I could get killed."

"The good Lord won't let that happen. Yes, I want us to get married."

"We could be apart for a long time. You might meet some-one else."

"So could you. Would you want that?"

"No! I love YOU!"

"And I love you. I can't imagine loving anyone else."

"But if you got pregnant, you'd be alone to have our baby…"

"Nothing would make me happier than carrying OUR baby…and my folks and your father are here…"

Jimmy smiled and held Annie at arm's length. "You are one stubborn woman. I don't know that I really want to marry anyone that stubborn."

"But you do. You really do."

"I guess I do. I'll tell you what. After I'm finished with Basic Training, I get two weeks leave before I have to report to wherever they're going to send me, probably Arizona. That's where most of the colored soldiers are ending up."

"I thought that if you were an American soldier it didn't make any difference what color you were."

"Oh, it makes a difference. A big difference! Coloreds and whites don't serve in the same units. Anyway, when I get that leave, if you still want to get married, I'm yours."

Jimmy dropped to one knee and took Annie's hand, "Annie May Culver, will you marry me?"

Annie jumped into Jimmy's arms, "Mr. Buck Private James Thompson, are you asking this woman to be your wedded wife?"

"Well, I think she's a little demented for wanting to marry a Buck Private heading off to war, but if that's what she wants…"

"I'll have everything all planned and pretty by the time you get back. I love you, Jimmy."

"And I love you. Now, I've got to go down to the factory and tell them where they can put their dirty dishes from now on."

"Jimmy, don't leave the company on bad terms. Remember, your Dad still works there."

"OK. I'll just tell them I'm quitting. I'm in the Army."

Charlie and Pete were talking as Jimmy approached.

"You think you'll be going into the Army, Pete?" Charlie asked, stomping out a half-smoked cigarette.

"Doesn't look like it. The draft board says I'm 4-F. Flat feet, asthma and too many dependents. Remember, I have a wife and four kids to take care of. You?"

"I was going to volunteer but my boss wants me to stay and get some new people trained. Either way, I expect my draft number to come up real soon. I want to get to the Pacific, kill me some of those Nips. How's the new Production line shaping up?"

"Not great. Tough getting good people in wartime, kids, women, coloreds. No one with any experience. Which reminds me, I'd better get back before something really bad happens."

As Pete walked away, he and Jimmy crossed paths. Pete looked at him, shook his head, and laughed.

"Throwing anymore rocks these days, Pete?" Jimmy asked.

Pete paused, and stared angrily, his face turning red. Not sure how to react, he spit at Jimmy's feet and walked away.

"Charlie!"

"Where the hell have you been the past few days?" Charlie said, not looking up.

"I've been kinda' busy."

Charlie turned, startled to see Jimmy in uniform. "Woo-eee. Look at the nigger all dressed up."

"I enlisted. I'm now Private James Thompson and I don't need to deal with your red neck bullshit anymore."

"Black son-of-a-bitch! Just proves what I always thought. If our government is going to build an Army of coloreds, the Germans might just win. My buddies and me better get in this war quick so 'we'all' can win it."

"I don't know. White sheets don't exactly go with khaki brown. But you and your friends can rest easy, us 'coloreds' will win the war and make it safe for you white folks."

"When it's all over and you come back to your dirty pots, you'll find that nothin's changed. You'll still be washing dishes."

Jimmy smiled, coming to attention, he slowly put on his cap, stomped his heels and faced Charlie.

"Maybe. Maybe not."

Smiling, Jimmy performed a formal military about-face and left a speechless Charlie staring.

Chapter Twenty-Six

Ira had taken a long lunch, walking in the park near *the Courier*. The leaves were just beginning to change and the heat from the sun was a little less intense as each day got a little shorter. It was refreshing to be out of the frenetic atmosphere that absorbed most of the working day. When he returned to the office, Erma was waiting to drop a stack of newspapers on his desk.

"I hate when people do that. I work at this desk. I like it clean, not cluttered. You do remember that I'm Managing Editor of this newspaper...and your boss...and..."

"...and dinner companion and..."

"OK! Enough! What is all this?"

"Some days the world looks better, and today is one of those days."

"Your date with Cory went well, I assume."

"What? No! That was weeks ago and he's off somewhere on the high seas."

"Then some other happy event. What could it be? I mean, you and I didn't spend last evening together."

"Funny! Are you ready? The first group of women have been inducted into the WACs and they're already arriving at Fort Des Moines, Iowa for their training."

"And?"

"AND the group contains 400 white women and 40 Colored women. Colored women and white women. In uniform! Serving together! It isn't much but it is a start."

"A good start. Do you think our Double V campaign had any impact?"

"I'm not sure, but it can't be coincidence that the ratio of white to black women is 'proportional.'"

"It is, isn't it?" Ira said, pleased that at least something seemed right.

"It is! Maybe we're opening people's minds to rethink prejudices they'd never questioned. Here look at these pictures from Iowa. Negro and White women training together."

"Are they sharing the same sleeping quarters?"

"No, but that will come eventually."

"Maybe."

"I'm an optimist."

"And a cute one. Let's get some profiles of the women. They're heroines. It would also help if we could get pictures and reactions from some of the white girls.

Erma wasted no time. She had come to work with a small suitcase and her train ticket in hand. She was getting familiar with transferring trains in Chicago. She decided to spend the night in Des Moines so she could arrive at the military post the following morning.

She arrived at the gate promptly at 8:00 a.m. and showed her Press pass to the guard. A few minutes later she was escorted to an office in a Quonset hut and greeted by a tall, stern looking woman, Lt. Nancy Bergstrom, mid-twenties, white, with a twangy western accent.

"Lt. Bergstrom, how do you do. I'm Erma Chandler, a reporter for the *Pittsburgh Courier*."

"Yes, Miss Chandler. I was told that you were to be granted access to the women for an article you're writing. It's good to have you here. I was told that the *Courier* is a Negro newspaper. I confess I didn't know there were Negro newspapers. I'm from Montana. We don't have a large colored population."

"There are several black owned newspapers spread across the country. *The Courier* is the largest. I'm excited to be here. Will I be able to talk to the women in training?"

"The colored women?"

"Both the colored and the white women, if that's possible."

"We'll have to see. The Army is still nervous about training white and black women in the same classroom at the same time. It hasn't been done before."

"I understand. Have there been any incidents?"

"No. Both groups have been a little stand-off-ish to one another. I guess they aren't sure what's expected of them."

"Well then, how shall we proceed?"

"I thought we could visit several of the classrooms this morning and you could chat with them in the afternoon, maybe have dinner with them. Does that sound all right?"

"Fine!"

The two women walked across the base stopping at a classroom where the recruits were learning how to operate a telegraph, learning Morse code. Erma took several pictures with her camera. Satisfied, Lt. Bergstrom led her to another part of the Fort to visit a motor pool.

Erma broke into a huge grin. Of all people she'd never expected to see was her old friend, Sarah. Large trucks were in various stages of maintenance, parts strewn everywhere.

White and black uniformed women were working when Sarah spotted Erma standing nearby watching her.

"Erma. Erma! Over her. It's Sarah."

"Sarah Blount? You? In the Army?"

"I enlisted. Imagine me, a WAC."

"Private Blount! Attention!" the Lieutenant demanded.

Sarah came to attention as Erma watched, impressed, but wondering how the Army had tamed her gregarious friend.

"Miss Chandler, you and Private Blount apparently know one another."

"Yes, Lieutenant. Sarah and I lived in the same boarding house when I first arrived in Pittsburgh."

"Small world! That's fine. Private, why don't you describe to your friend what it is you're learning?"

"Yes, sir. Erma, take off your coat and jacket. I wouldn't want it to get dirty. We're learning to take care of these trucks we'll be driving."

"Private, I'll leave Miss Chandler in your hands. Show her around and plan on joining us for dinner in the Mess Hall at 1700. Understood?"

"Yes, ma'am."

"Erma, if that's agreeable, I'll see you at dinner," she said, turning and leaving without waiting for Erma to respond.

"Come closer, Erma. You see this. This is the carburetor and this..."

Sarah disconnected one of the hoses and oil squirted out, drenching Erma and everyone near her. When she pulled back, her face and clothes were black with grease. Both women shrieked.

Several of the other women, white and black, laughed. Pretty soon everyone was laughing. One of the white girls went and got cleaning materials. She tried to help Sarah and

188

Erma get clean but it wasn't going to work. The entire group made suggestions on what to do.

"Guys, this is Erma Chandler. She's now a big-time reporter for the *Pittsburgh Courier*. We lived next to one another, even double-dated a few times."

"Hi, everyone. I hadn't planned on making this kind of impression."

"Sarah, you're some friend. The two of you are still covered with a lot of grease," Penny from New York chimed in.

Sally, a white girl from Virginia spoke up, "Did you bring a change of clothes?"

"No. It was supposed to be an up and back trip."

"Take off your skirt and blouse. We're about the same size. I can get the Supply Sergeant to replace mine. You can clean mine when you get home and send them back. I won't be wearing them for a while."

"That's so sweet. Thank you. Where you from?"

"Richmond! My name is Sally, Sally Pinfor."

"Thank you, again. Grease isn't my favorite color."

A gum-chewing red head, with a face filled with freckles, spoke up, "What are you doing here, anyway?"

"I'm here to do a story about black and white women training together. Any thoughts?"

"Well, when I'm covered with grease, I'm not sure which I am or that it matters." The mental picture of the girls covered in grease brought laughter from all of them.

"What do they call you?" Erma asked.

"They call me Red but my name is Hermione. That's why I'm glad they call me Red."

"Where are you from, Red?"

"Nashville, home of the Grand Ol' Opry. You like country music?"

189

"Love it."

"And, for the record, you're white, trust me," Sally clarified.

"You sure?"

"I'm sure," she said grinning.

"Where are the rest of you from?"

They chimed in, Los Angeles, Jacksonville, Albuquerque. And their reasons for joining ranged from having to leave home, to doing something important, to no idea.

"So, how's the training going? You girls all get along?"

"More than a hundred women who don't know one another. What could possibly go wrong?"

"As in 'black - white' wrong?"

"Black, white, city, country..."

"East, west, south...we're just all different. Most of us had never traveled anywhere."

"I know what that feels like. When I moved to Pittsburgh from a small town, the largest store I'd ever seen was a Woolworth's Five and Dime."

"And some of us went to college, others never finished high school."

"I hope the WACS didn't think we'd all be one size just because we put on uniforms, which I might add, never fit."

"And, I think Maxine's lipstick color is all wrong for her."

"And Sarah wears too much mascara."

"Race is just one difference. We're learning to focus on the job we have to do and ignore everything else."

The conversation continued to well past the time to meet for dinner but no one wanted to leave. Wondering where Erma was, Lt. Bergstrom went looking and heard the entire group laughing, chatting like old friends. She joined them.

Chapter Twenty-Seven

A few days later Ira was enjoying his second cup of coffee. He walked over to the ever-busy teletype. Wendall was there, scanning the ever-constant news flashes coming in from all over the world.

"Anyone who bet that this war was going to be over any time soon would have lost his shirt."

"At least we seem to have slowed the Japanese advance in the Pacific and Rommel in North Africa," Wendall noted.

"Maybe, but here it is, 1942 winding down and bad news is beating good news three to one.

Frank Bolden approached. "Ira, I think there's someone here to see you."

"Byron, come in. You're alone? Where is our bulldog friend from the FBI?"

"I escaped his clutches. He's probably picking up Hoover's dry cleaning."

"How'd you get here so early from Washington?"

"I came up yesterday from Philly and hopped an early train this morning."

"Come into my office. It's always good to see you, especially after the last visit."

"Yes, that wasn't much fun."

Ira stared out his window as Byron Price removed his coat and made himself comfortable.

"I love the fall weather, don't you?" Ira asked casually. "Leaves changing. A bite in the air. Sometimes I find myself walking to the office in the morning. Way too far to make sense but I start out and keep going."

"I've been doing the same in D.C. Surrounded by all that history. At least once a week I'd get some coffee and sit on the steps of the Lincoln Memorial. When I ran the Associated Press, life was busy but it was simpler. Find the story. Send a reporter to cover it. Report the facts. No subjectivity. Opinions stayed on the Editorial pages."

"That sounds as if the *Courier* is going to be censored, one way or the other, for its Double V campaign."

"I won't deny it was close. The lawyers at the Attorney General's office, under pressure from Hoover, were almost finished drafting the indictments. He kept up his drum beat that you were running a subversive organization."

"And?"

"And I'd like a drink to celebrate."

"What are we celebrating?"

"The President and the Congress have approved the principal of Proportional Representation. You've won an important victory, Ira."

Ira stared, stunned. Tears in his eyes, his voice weak, "They've accepted Proportional Representation?"

"They have. And, the government will now encourage the full participation of the Negro population in the war effort. Congratulations, Ira. Sincerely. You and the *Courier* have won an important victory and I wanted to bring this information to you personally."

Ira's voice choked up, "Thank you, Byron. I've still got time to insert a new headline. And I need to share this with the staff, Erma, Frank, Wendall and the rest of our people."

Frank, Wendall, Paul, and Tom rushed into Ira's office, everyone talking at the same time.

"It just came over the wire. The entire Tuskegee squadron is heading for England for combat training."

"They'll be flying the Air Force's newest fighter, the P-51 Mustang."

"Byron, did you know about this? Guys, I think you've all met Byron Price."

"Yes. Seems as if someone got their head out of their ass and did an entire reappraisal of what Negroes could contribute. Roosevelt even got the Southern states to concede that it was necessary, although I'm sure they bargained for something in exchange."

"Byron," Frank Bolden smiled, "You keep coming back here with good news and we'll get you your own desk."

"Byron was here to give us other good news. The government has adopted the principal of Proportional Representation. Negroes will now be full participants in the war."

Laughter and disbelief fill the room, also relief. There was no longer a threat that the *Courier* would be censured and shut down.

"One more thing brought me to Pittsburgh. I'm hoping it will make you all happy as well," Byron Price smiled as the room turned silent.

"I'm on a cloud at the moment floating on balloons. It would take a lot to bring me down," Ira said.

"Frank, we've approved your request to be a War Correspondent. You'll be one of only two Negro reporters with that designation. We want one in the Pacific theatre and the other in Europe. Since you're sort of the elder statesman, you get to choose."

"Saki or Schnapps? That's a difficult decision, Byron, but thank you," Frank said, clasping Byron's hand in gratitude.

"I'm thrilled for you, Frank," Ira smiled. "You'll do a terrific job. And don't forget, send us the stories first."

"And where is Erma?" Byron asked. "I'd like to say hi to her before I head back to D.C."

"Yes, our modest, young, female reporter had this Double V bone between her teeth and wouldn't let go. She needs to be here. She deserves a lot of the credit."

"Where is she?" Frank asked.

"She was on assignment, interviewing WACS at Fort Des Moines. But she was due back here a couple of hours ago. We should all have a drink to celebrate before you go, Byron. We can watch the sunset together and dream of better times."

As the team congratulated one another, Erma appeared in the doorway a few minutes later. She was wearing a coat. "Did I hear my name mentioned? I'd like one of those drinks as well. I heard the news. We should drink a toast to Jimmy Thompson. Who thought that a Letter to the Editor would lead to this? Here's to you, Jimmy."

Everyone stood and joined in the toast. Wendall helped Erma take off her coat and the entire room froze in place. Erma was wearing an army uniform.

Ira was the first to react. "What's going on? What have you done?"

"I enlisted in the Women's Army Auxiliary Corps."

"You were only supposed to get interviews, do a story."

"Ira, they were such an enthusiastic group of women and what they're doing is important and..."

"But you're a reporter."

"After the Double V campaign and everything we've been writing, I couldn't let it be someone else's war. I needed to be a part of it."

"But you can't go, I need you."

"You'll find another woman reporter."

"No! I need **YOU!**"

"Oh, Ira. That ship has sailed. I love you. Maybe it was a young girl's crush. I don't know. But, like Jimmy Thompson, I need to get into this war and make a difference."

"You made a difference here. The Double V campaign might not have existed without you."

"I also believe in its message. And, I'm not angry about us. We just wanted different things."

"Well, we're all proud of you," Wendall chimed in.

"And you look terrific. Like a black Lana Turner" Tom laughed."

How about like a black Erma Chandler?" Byron Price said, raising his glass in salute.

"Private Erma Chandler, United States Women's Army Auxiliary."

More than one million Negroes served valiantly in World War II!

James G. Thompson's letter to the Pittsburgh Courier proposing Double V

(Jan. 31, 1942)

Like all true Americans, my greatest desire at this time, this crucial point of our history; is a desire for a complete victory over the forces of evil, which threaten our existence today. Behind that desire is also a desire to serve, this, my country, in the most advantageous way. Most of our leaders are suggesting that we sacrifice every other ambition to the paramount one, victory. With this I agree; but I also wonder if another victory could not be achieved at the same time. After all, the things that beset the world now are basically the same things which upset the equilibrium of nations internally, states, counties, cities, homes and even the individual. Being an American of dark complexion and some 26 years, these questions flash through my mind: "Should I sacrifice my life to live half American?" "Will things be better for the next generation in the peace to follow?" "Would it be demanding

199

too much to demand full citizenship rights in exchange for the sacrificing of my life." "Is the kind of America I know worth defending?" "Will America be a true and pure democracy after this war?" "Will colored Americans suffer still the indignities that have been heaped upon them in the past?" These and other questions need answering; I want to know, and I believe every colored American, who is thinking, wants to know. This may be the wrong time in to broach such subjects, but haven't all good things obtained by men been secured through sacrifice during just such times of strife? I suggest that while we keep defense and victory in the forefront that we don't lose sight of our fight for true democracy at home. The "V for Victory" sign is being displayed prominently all so-called democratic countries which are fighting for victory over aggression, slavery and tyranny. If this V sign means that to those now engaged in this great conflict then let colored Americans adopt the double VV for a double victory—The first V for victory over our enemies from without, the second V for victory over our enemies within. For surely those who perpetrate these ugly prejudices here are seeing to destroy our democratic form of government just as surely as the Axis forces. This should not and would not lessen our efforts to bring this conflict to a successful conclusion; but should and would make us stronger to resist these evil forces which threaten us. America could become united as never before and become truly the home of democracy. In way of an answer to the foregoing questions in a preceding paragraph, I might say that there is no doubt that this country is worth defending; things will be different for the next generation; colored Americans will come into their own, and America will eventually become the true democracy it was designed to be. These things will become a reality in time;

but not through any relaxation of the efforts to secure them. In conclusion let me say that though these questions often permeate my mind, I love American and am willing to die for the America I know will someday become a reality.

ACKNOWLEDGEMENTS

My deepest gratitude goes to those who helped by reading, suggesting, and correcting my manuscript, my tendency to overuse the past pluperfect tense, and a forgetfulness at inserting commas. Professor Patrick Washburn, Lauren Silinsky, Kali Harrison, and Jeff Maxwell have all been wonderful in giving their time and encouragement and if errors still remain, they are mine.

Mostly, all of us owe our thanks to James Thompson, Erma Chandler, and Ira Lewis for their bravery in addressing our country's ongoing battle with racism.

About the Author

Carole Eglash-Kosoff lives and writes in Valley Village, California. She graduated from UCLA and spent her career teaching, writing, and traveling to more than eighty countries. She was Controller and Chief Financial Officer of several apparel companies and owner of the only button manufacturing plant in the Western United States.

In 2006, following the death of her husband, mother, and brother within a month, she spent several months teaching in the black townships of South Africa, the origin of her first book, **The Human Spirit – Apartheid's Unheralded Heroes.**

Over the next decade, while writing the books listed below, Mrs. Eglash-Kosoff wrote and produced four stage plays, including the Ovation award winning, **When Jazz Had the Blues**.

Check out her website: www.caroleeglashkosoff.com
Contact: ceglash@aol.com

Other books by Carole Eglash-Kosoff:

THE HUMAN SPIRIT
—Apartheid's Unheralded Heroes

ISBN #978-1-4520-3306-8 (Softback)

More information is available on the website:

www.thehumanspirit-thebook.com
YouTube: http://youtu.be/T-LgBG-4tX4

Prologue

Apartheid in South Africa has now been gone more than fifteen years but the heroes of their struggle to achieve a Black majority-run democracy are still being revealed. Some individuals toiled publicly, but most worked tirelessly in the shadows to improve the welfare of the Black and Colored populations that had been so neglected. Nelson Mandela was still in prison; clean water and sanitation barely existed; AIDS was beginning to orphan an entire generation.

Meanwhile a white, Jewish, middle class woman, joined with Tutu, Millie, Ivy, Zora and other concerned Black women, respectfully called Mamas, to help those most in need, often being beaten and arrested by white security police.

This book tells the story of these women and others who have spent their adult lives making South Africa a better place for those who were the country's most disadvantaged.

When Stars Align

ISBN#978-1-4567-3890-7 (Softback)

More information is available on the website:
www.whenstarsalign-thebook.com

Prologue

The love that Thaddeus and Amy feel for one another can get them both killed. He is colored, an ex-slave, and she is white. In 19th century Louisiana mixed race relationships are both illegal and unacceptable.

Moss Grove, a large Mississippi River cotton plantation has thrived from the use of slave labor while its owners lived lives of comfort and privilege. Thaddeus, born more than a decade earlier from the rape of a young field slave by the heir to the plantation, is raised as a Moss Grove house servant. His presence remains a thorn in the side of the man who sired him.

Deepening divisiveness between North and South launches the Civil War and changes Moss Grove in ways no one could have anticipated. With the war swirling we see the battles and carnage through Thaddeus' eyes. The war ends and he returns to Moss Grove and to Amy, hoping to enjoy their newly won freedoms. With the help of Union soldiers, schools are established to educate those who were formerly prohibited from learning to read. Medical clinics are opened and businesses begun. Black legislators are elected and help to pass new laws. Hope flourishes. Perhaps the stars will now finally align for the young lovers.

In 1876, however, the ex-Confederate states barter the selection of President Rutherford B. Hayes for removal of all Union troops from their soil in the most contested election in American history. Within a decade hopes are dashed as Jim Crow laws are passed, the Ku Klux Klan launches new violence, and black progress is crushed.

'When Stars Align' is a soaring novel of memorable white, Negro, and colored men and women set against actual historic events.

****

Winds Of Change

ISBN#978-0-9839601-0-2 (Softback)
ISBN#978-0-9839601-1-9 (eBook)

More information is available on the website:

www.windsofchange-thebook.com

Prologue

The racially charged love and conflict of the critically acclaimed *When Stars Align* become more entrenched after the Civil War and Reconstruction. Amy had taken her daughter, nephew, and a son she'd had never been able to acknowledge, born from her love with Thaddeus, her colored lover, to San Francisco, as a refuge from the intense racial scrutiny of the South.

They are forced to return to their old home, Moss Grove, a successful Mississippi River cotton plantation, as young adults. They discover facts about themselves that refute everything they believed regarding both their parents and their racial background. It changes the lives of each of them. Bess and Stephen's love is thwarted. Josiah struggles with echoes of his past.

It is a tumultuous time in American history that includes the inventions of airplanes, automobiles, telephones and movies midst decades of lynching's and economic turmoil. It is the Spanish-American War and World War I. Racial biases complicate lives and relationships as newly arrived immigrants vie with white and Negro workers all trying to gain a piece of the American dream. **Winds of Change** is a soaring historic fiction novel that stands alone but follows the next generation from those we came to know in *When Stars Align into the 20th century*. It is a socially relevant, historically accurate, saga of decades often overlooked in American history.

BY ONE VOTE

ISBN#978-0-9839601-2-6
Published by Valley Village Publishing
2012
www.byonevote-thebook.com

We live in a period of economic and political unrest and we believe it to be worse than at any time in our history...but it isn't. America's two hundred plus years of existence has been one of turmoil, dissension, and war. It has been a time of economic growth and stagnation. Each decade has found stalwarts and dissenters convinced that they, alone, have the best solution for the country's ills.

A surprising number of events that altered the country's direction resulted from the vote of a single individual either in support of a change or opposed to it. Names such as James Bayard, Edmund Ross, and Joseph Bradley are unknown but they altered the fabric or our nation as significantly as more famous Americans. This book, *By One*

Vote, tells these stories. The events are factual, the drama-
tizations surrounding them are the studied imagination of
the author.

View a summary of the book on You tube: http://youtu
.be/tIDBJc7JUEQ

SEX, DRUGS, & FASHION

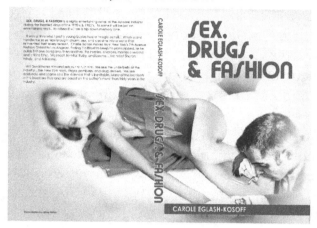

Registered WGA West #1676121
Registered Library of Congress Copyright 1-992378771
Cover designed by James Kirtley

Website: www.sexdrugsandfashion-thebook.com

13-Digit ISBN:978-0-9839601-4-0 (e-book)
13-Digit ISBN:978-0-9839601-1-9 (Softback)

SEX, DRUGS, & FASHION is a highly entertaining novel of the Apparel industry during the frenzied days of the 1970's & 1980's. To some it will be just an enjoyable story. To others it will be a trip down memory lane.

Charlie Barron, growing up in New York's 7th Avenue Fashion District, moves to Los Angeles and its embryonic environment. He finds it difficult to keep his pants zipped as he builds first one company, then another, always at odds with his business partners. His first partner, Pablo, is from

El Salvador, where garments can be made less expensively. Everything goes well until that country's revolution closes the factory. Meanwhile Pablo's marriage crumbles as his gay life style is revealed. Charlie's second partner, Neil Pastore, is an Italian Jew who owns a fabric company. Charlie marries, divorces, marries a second and a third time. We meet Jennifer, Ruby, and Lorena. We meet Sharon, Windy, and Adrienne.

The novel also deals with the underbelly of the industry... the New York mob, Vegas gamblers, and cocaine dealers. We see kickbacks and scams. You'll meet Will Duval who has competed with Charlie for decades, always preferring short-cuts to success. Their competition often leads to violence.

Most of the characters in the book are composites of people the author knew and the significant events are based on the authors more than thirty years in the industry.

CPSIA information can be obtained
at www.ICGtesting.com
Printed in the USA
LVHW081341210321
682028LV00046B/1452